JAN 2 3 20

D0546263

NAPA COUNTY LIBRARY
580 COOMBS STREET
NAPA, CA 94559

ALSO BY RIAD SATTOUF

The Arab of the Future, Volume 1:
A Childhood in the Middle East, 1978–1984

The Arab of the Future, Volume 2:
A Childhood in the Middle East, 1984–1985

The Arab of the Future, Volume 3
A Childhood in the Middle East, 1985–1987

THE ARAB
OF THE FUTURE 4

A GRAPHIC MEMOIR

A Childhood in the Middle East (1987–1992)

RIAD SATTOUF

TRANSLATED BY SAM TAYLOR

METROPOLITAN BOOKS   HENRY HOLT AND COMPANY   NEW YORK

Metropolitan Books
Henry Holt and Company
Publishers since 1866
120 Broadway
New York, New York 10271

Metropolitan Books® and m® are registered trademarks of
Macmillan Publishing Group, LLC.

Copyright © 2019
Translation copyright © 2019 by Sam Taylor
All rights reserved.
Distributed in Canada by Raincoast Book Distribution Limited

Originally published in France in 2018 by Allary Éditions

Riad Sattouf warmly thanks Charline Bailot for her amazing work on this book.

Library of Congress Cataloging-in-Publication data for the first volume is as follows:

Sattouf, Riad, author.
    [Arabe du futur. English]
  The Arab of the future : growing up in the Middle East (1978–1984) : a graphic memoir / Riad Sattouf ;
translated from the French by Sam Taylor.
      pages cm
  ISBN 978-1-62779-344-5 (hardback)—ISBN (invalid) 978-1-62779-345-2 (electronic book)
  1. Sattouf, Riad—Childhood and youth—Comic books, strips, etc. 2. Cartoonists—France—Biography—
Comic books, strips, etc. 3. Middle East—Biography—Comic books, strips, etc. 4. Graphic novels.
I. Taylor, Sam, 1970– translator. II. Title.
  NC1499.S337A2 2015
  741.5'69092–dc23
  [B]   2014041152

ISBN: 978-1-250-15066-0

Our books may be purchased in bulk for promotional, educational, or business use. Please contact your
local bookseller or the Macmillan Corporate and Premium Sales Department at (800) 221-7945, extension
5442, or by e-mail at MacmillanSpecialMarkets@macmillan.com.

First U.S. Edition 2019

Designed by Kelly S. Too
Typography and composition by Jonathan Bennett

Printed in China
10 9 8 7 6 5 4 3 2 1

CHAPTER 1

My name is Riad. In 1988, I was about to turn ten and I was pretty cute.

Wavy light-brown hair →

← Head a bit too big for my body

Skinny →

← Sleepy eyes

A bit smug →

← Acid-washed jeans

My father had just taken a new job as associate professor in modern history at the University of Riyadh in Saudi Arabia . . .

SAUDI ARABIA? NEVER!

WE'RE NOT GOING!

He wanted us to come with him, but my mother refused.

IT'S THE WORST COUNTRY IN THE WORLD! If you steal something, they cut off your hand!

If you accidentally poke out your neighbor's eye, they gouge out your eye, too!

Are you sure? That sounds a bit much.

She took us to France, close to her mother's house. All of us—me, my mother, and my brothers, Yahya and Fadi—lived in Cap Fréhel.

There's nothing worse in that country than being a woman!

You're not allowed out of the house unless you cover up every inch of your body and you're accompanied by a man! Can you imagine?

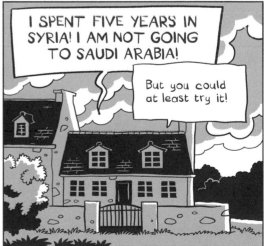

I SPENT FIVE YEARS IN SYRIA! I AM NOT GOING TO SAUDI ARABIA!

But you could at least try it!

And it's better for the children to be with their father.

It's better to be a family.

I agree! BUT ONLY IN FRANCE!

That's what I told Abdel.

He chose to go anyway. It's his choice.

Mama, look at the Barbarian.

In Saudi Arabia, when a woman's put in prison and she's finished her sentence, the prison calls for a man in her family to come and fetch her!

And he can come whenever he wants! It's the men who decide when she gets out! And most of them just leave the women in prison forever, to get rid of them!!! THEY NEVER GET OUT!

I read that in a magazine!!!

But why would you be in prison?

You never know, with my luck. A miscarriage of justice...

Ha!

I want the children to go to school in France. AND THAT'S FINAL!

Okay, okay!

Hmph!

It had been six months since I last saw my father.

We didn't have a phone. Sometimes he'd call my grandmother's house.

Oh look, that's a pretty dress...

We had to wait by the phone at a certain time.

RING

It rang once. That meant we had to call him back.

Ah, it's Scrooge.

He didn't want to pay for the call.

My parents went at each other for a few minutes, always about the same things.

No, I don't care if there are French supermarkets!

I wouldn't live in that horrible country if you paid me ten million francs!

Oh, and you need to send more money.

After that, my mother would call to my brothers to talk...

Come on, it's Papa.

Hello, Papa?

Who dat? Who dat, Mama?

...then it was my turn.

Riad! Come talk to your father!

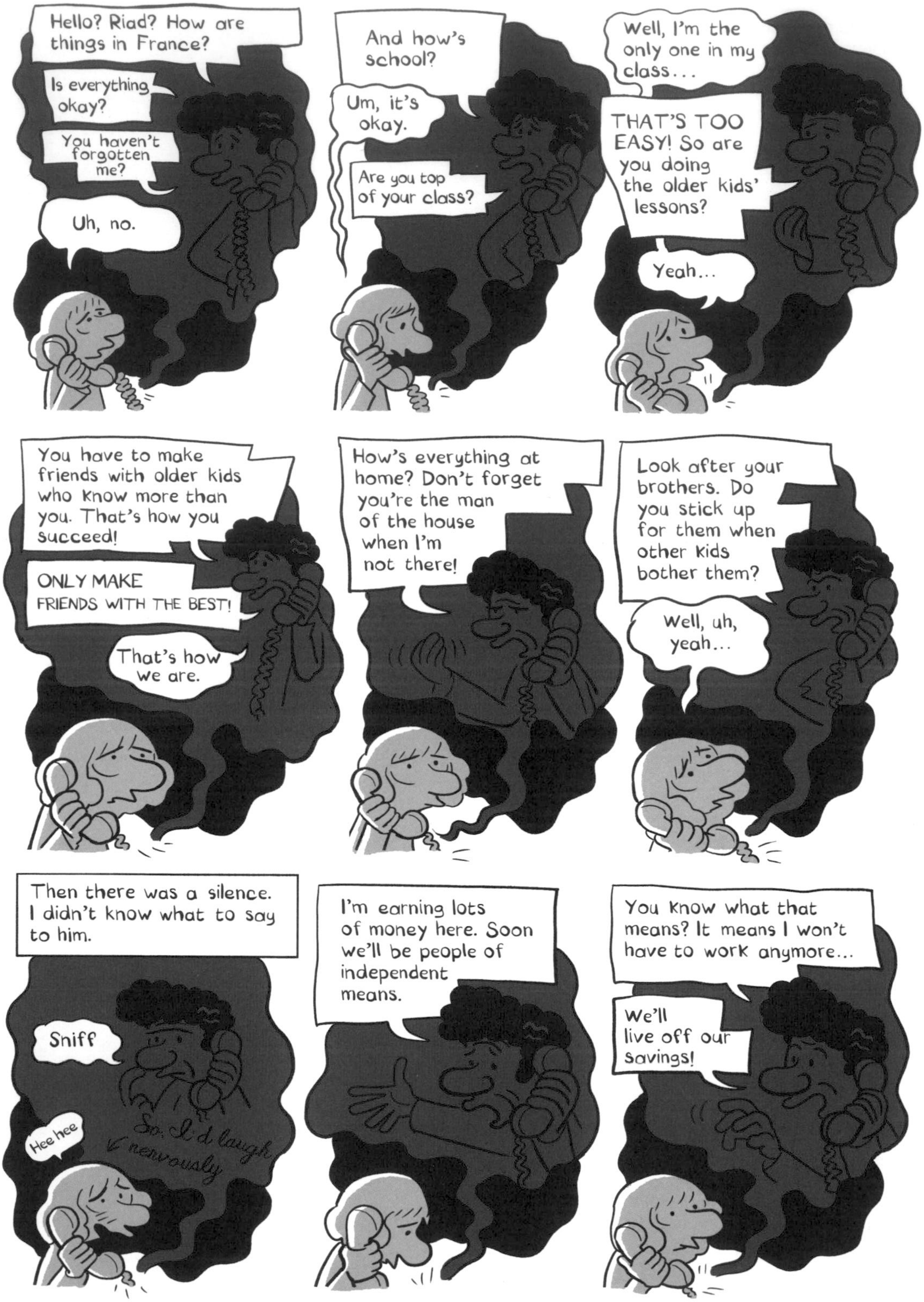
Hello? Riad? How are things in France?
Is everything okay?
You haven't forgotten me?
Uh, no.
And how's school?
Um, it's okay.
Are you top of your class?
Well, I'm the only one in my class...
THAT'S TOO EASY! So are you doing the older kids' lessons?
Yeah...
You have to make friends with older kids who know more than you. That's how you succeed!
ONLY MAKE FRIENDS WITH THE BEST!
That's how we are.
How's everything at home? Don't forget you're the man of the house when I'm not there!
Look after your brothers. Do you stick up for them when other kids bother them?
Well, uh, yeah...
Then there was a silence. I didn't know what to say to him.
Sniff
Hee hee
So, I'd laugh nervously
I'm earning lots of money here. Soon we'll be people of independent means.
You know what that means? It means I won't have to work anymore...
We'll live off our savings!

Then he would talk to me in Arabic.

I barely understood a word.

Well, not much...

Shu? Am tedross mnih drouss el arabi?

Riad! Are you studying Arabic?

Are you reading your Arabic textbooks?

Um...

You have to! It's your mother tongue! In Libya your Arabic was better than your **French**!

I'm going to send you some workbooks!!! All those years at school in Syria! And you've already forgotten it all?

YOU'RE AN ARAB! AN ARAB, YOU HEAR?

Um, okay! So... here's Mama!

Bye, Papa.

But you—

Then he would talk about me to my mother.

Yes, his grades are good. But they don't do marks out of 20 anymore.

It's A, B, C...

He's in elementary school. That's how it is in France...

You don't know that?

I felt strangely relieved at the thought that it would be a few weeks before we spoke to him again.

Well, no. I can't teach him Arabic! I DON'T SPEAK ARABIC! What do you expect me to do? If you were here, you could force him...

I DON'T SPEAK ARABIC! WHAT PART OF THAT DON'T YOU UNDERSTAND?

After that, we'd go home.

It had been hard finding a place to live in Cap Fréhel. There were no long-term rentals.

The mayor put us in touch with some people who owned a vacation home in the village.

They let us rent it on one condition

We had to move out when they came there on vacation.

Can I have the Kinder Egg that Grandma gave me?

Sure.

Since my grandmother was only about 500 yards away, my mother agreed to the terms.

Me too?

Yes!

We'd never see the owners, and the rent was very cheap.

My father sent us 2500 francs a month. We lived on that.

Hey! A new toy for my collection!

We didn't have a car, so we went everywhere on foot.

My mother was looking for work. She wrote letters all day long.

There must be something. Surely someone around here needs a secretary.

But there was no work in the area.

I'll apply to 300 jobs!

Nobody gets rejected 300 times!

This was my father's plan: he would earn lots of money in Saudi Arabia.

Let's see what's on TV.

And come to France when he was rich. Then we would buy a house...

Oh, I'm so tired.

...and we'd stay there for good.

I like the flowers on this show...

YAWWWN!

I wish someone would give me a bouquet like that one day...

My mother enrolled me in the village school, where there was one class for second through fifth grade. I was the only fourth-grader.

Yaouen and Loïc, who I knew in kindergarten, were fifth-graders.

One day, the teacher said:

If you have any questions about anything at all, just ask me! There's no such thing as a silly question.

I'm no scientist, but I know a little bit about a lot of things!

So I spent my days asking her questions.

Miss! When did the dinosaurs live?

Miss! What's a cosine?

Miss! Are there snakes in Brittany?

I wanted to know the answers, but I also wanted the teacher to think I was smart.

Um, I think there are grass snakes here...

Not sure about adders...

She never told me I was getting on her nerves.

Miiiiss! Why is the sky blue?

I had very good grades, and I always finished my work before the others.

Miiiiiss! I've finished. Can I draw?

Yes! Go ahead!

I was obsessed with drawing shadows.

I wanted them to be perfect

The third-grade girls were impressed by my drawings.

Wow! That's really good!

That's the best drawing I've ever seen!

Sabrina, back to your seat.

Miss! Do you like my drawing?

It's not bad. A little too gory for my taste...

...You should take classes if you want to improve.

Annoyed, because I felt sure I was already a pro.

"Oh, look how great my drawings are, blah blah blah!"

I told my dad about you and he said you're just a big fat show-off!

Heh heh, that's what he said, yeah. So, there!

YAOUEN! FOCUS ON YOUR WORK!

RIAD! YOU TOO!

I really liked going to my grandmother's house.

WOOOOOO OO OO

It was very dark inside, like it was haunted . . .

. . . but also cozy and comforting.

RIAD! You have mail!

The only things my grandmother read were *Paris Match* and the TV guide . . .

Inside the TV guide were ads for children's magazines. She signed me up for lots of them.

Animal cards (excellent)

Books about different cultures (awesome) →

A news magazine for children (not so great)

REAL LIFE IN POMPEI

THE CHILDRENS TIMES

SCALLOP SPONGE
FENNEC FOX
FINBACK WHALE

She loved to watch me read these things.

Grandma! Did you know there are no anacondas in Brittany? Only in Amazonia!

Oh really? Interesting.

Genuinely curious →

Read it all carefully, my love! You don't want to end up like me or the people around here!

We're just stupid YOKELS!

We wasted our lives!

YOU HAVE TO BE SOMEONE!

"The ferret is a domesticated carnivorous mammal that lives . . ."

My grandmother's main activity was cooking. She was obsessed with food.

And here are the scallops!

Tell me what you think.

AAAH AAAH

She always seemed to be starving.

I used breadcrumbs, but they didn't brown properly!

I hope they're okay.

Chomp

Chomp

Chomp

Fresh like the sea

Perfect.

Charles complimented her in a calm, serious voice that showed he understood how important it was to her.

Most relieved person in world

Then it was our turn.

Excellent!

REALLY YUMMY, GRANDMA!

I want a Petit Suisse!

When we all praised her, she radiated happiness.

During the war we didn't have scallops, you know!

All we had to eat were artichokes!

Artichokes! Ugh, just thinking about them makes me feel sick!

Mmm! These scallops really **are** good!

My mother's father came to see us from time to time.

Nice little house!

Abdel should buy one just like it!

COME ON! LET'S ALL GO TO THE SUPERMARKET!

I'M BUYING!

My grandfather was very generous. He liked to make us happy.

You like that plane? It's yours!

It's not a plane, it's a space shuttle!

Well, it's still yours!

He too was obsessed with food and often talked about the German occupation.

Look at all those aisles full of rice and pasta!

You should have seen us in '43 ...

Stock up! Let's get enough for a few weeks!

I was a young boy during the war. At night I'd sometimes be woken up by voices.

But they weren't really voices! It was the sound of my stomach gurgling! Can you imagine?

Pssst! Riad! Check out that babe!

WHAT A PIECE OF ASS.

He was always going on about girls. I had the feeling he expected something from me.

You put your hand on her tights and then you slide it up—so good!

And if she has big breasts...

But no matter how much I looked, I couldn't see what was so exciting about a woman's legs.

Reality

What I saw

This began to seriously worry him.

So, do you have any girl-friends?

Pick a girl at school, drag her to a corner, and kiss her on the mouth!

That's what boys do!

Papa, leave him alone!

Ugh! What about you? How are the girls in kindergarten?

I have a girlfriend.

There you go! That's my boy!

?!?

My mother didn't get many replies to her job applications, and the ones she did get were just rejections.

We need jobs! What a bunch of crooks!

President Mitterrand is on the campaign trail. Today he was in Rennes...

We watched TV all day long.

My grandparents had aged a lot

Look at that, it's raining cats and dogs!

Oh, it won't last...

Aroma of herbal tea and wood smoke

Who is that old woman? AHH! It's Michèle Morgan!!! And she used to be so beautiful!

DING DONG

It's the mailman! Why's he ringing the doorbell?

AH!

It's for me!

Huh? You ordered something?

Surpriiiise!

?!

Go on, open it!

It's for you!

Really?

HAUT
BAS

BAS

WOOF

Charles had ordered a Westie through the mail. The dog breeder's daughter had packaged it and, without telling her father, put some butter in the box so the puppy wouldn't be hungry during its journey. So he came to us covered in grease.

Oh, what a cute little buttery dog!

He'll amuse us!

Let's call him Moustik!

That's good!

Ah, little Moustik

He's a Scottish breed! They hunt foxes!

They're trained to burrow down their holes!

THEY'RE KILLERS!

But very cute!

There was also a photo of two angry-looking dogs.

They're Moustik's parents! It says here he has four brothers and sisters.

He'll never see them again?

Well, no! We're his family now. That's why we have to be extra nice to him. He's a poor little orphan dog!

I liked spending time with Charles.

He was very gentle and never made me do anything, unlike my father.

Where did I put that thing...

Ah, here it is!

Smell of dried cobwebs

He was always finding old things to show me.

This is a stereoscope from the end of the last century. It belonged to my father.

He owned a factory. He was VERY rich. He had a stereo photo taken of our house.

This is the only one I have left.

You put the glass slide in here...

...and you look.

That little boy you see is me! In 1920. I was five years old.

He looked like me in black and white.

My father was crazy about new technologies! He had a lot of money. He was one of the first people to buy a car...

Then, in 1929, when I was 14, there was a stock market crash, and my father lost EVERYTHING! We had been rich, but after that we were poor.

PSHH!

Would I, one day, be old like him?

Crack!

Charles never yelled at me.

It doesn't matter! Let me sweep up the bits of glass so you don't hurt yourself.

You'll be the last person who saw me as a child!

♪

Charles loved sports. He enrolled me in a soccer club for children in a nearby town called Matignon.

I was very excited.

There's nothing better than team sports!

Will I get good quickly?

Oh yes! Soccer is like anything else—it just takes practice!

My grandparents bought me expensive gear.

Bright blue T-shirt

Soccer cleats

White shorts

I had everything I needed for my first session.

We'll pick him up in an hour!

Come on, Riad! You can go to the changing room with the others.

I went into a room where some boys were getting changed.

Smell of feet

I sat on the bench and opened my bag.

Hey, that's my spot!

Move!

That's your spot, over there.

FAG SITS HERE

Fag? I hope that doesn't mean I'm playing defender...

26

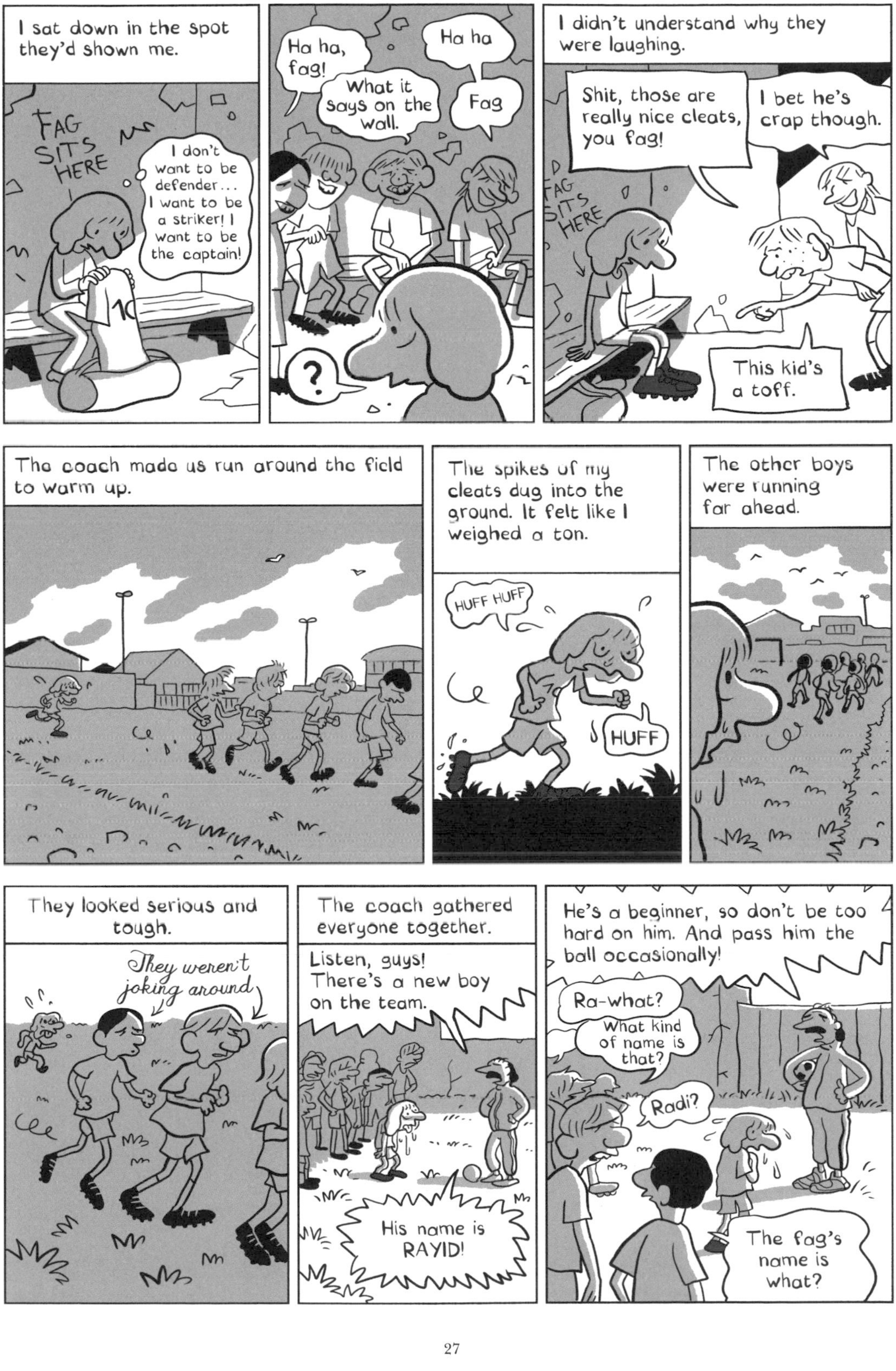
I sat down in the spot they'd shown me.
FAG SITS HERE
I don't want to be defender... I want to be a striker! I want to be the captain!
10
Ha ha, fag!
What it says on the wall.
Ha ha
Fag
?
I didn't understand why they were laughing.
Shit, those are really nice cleats, you fag!
I bet he's crap though.
FAG SITS HERE
This kid's a toff.
The coach made us run around the field to warm up.
The spikes of my cleats dug into the ground. It felt like I weighed a ton.
HUFF HUFF
HUFF
The other boys were running far ahead.
They looked serious and tough.
They weren't joking around
The coach gathered everyone together.
Listen, guys! There's a new boy on the team.
His name is RAYID!
He's a beginner, so don't be too hard on him. And pass him the ball occasionally!
Ra-what?
What kind of name is that?
Radi?
The fag's name is what?

After that, we practiced penalty kicks.

We had to kick the ball as hard as possible into the net.

BAM!

These guys were firing cannonballs.

My turn came.

HMF!

NO BIG DEAL, RAYID! NEXT!

So? Did you enjoy it? Are you the new Platini?

YEAH YEAH!

...and also I was wondering...what does "fag" mean?

Where did you hear that word?

You mustn't say that! It's horrible!

"Fag is an insulting term."

It's for homosexuals. That means people who engage in sexual activity with...

WILL YOU STOP?!

Well, he asked. I was just explaining.

...so, basically, it's men or boys who love other men or boys.

SHUT UP! SHUT UP!

Where did you hear that word?

Um, someone on the TV said it.

You must never say it! It's a terrible word!

There's NOTHING worse than homosexuals!

Sabrina and Gwenaëlle, two third-grade girls, would often smile at me.

Sometimes they'd giggle too

I didn't know how to react.

So I'd make my Conan the Barbarian face

Hee hee hee

Psst! Read this! It's for you! And then pass it on to Yaouen

and Loïc! It's from the girls in the class.

Most handsome boys in the class
1 Riad (nice hair)
2 Yaouen
3 Loïc
4 Sébastien

Hey! This is from Sabrina and Gwenaëlle!

Hee hee

It made me happy, even if I wasn't surprised: I was so handsome.

Yaouen and Loïc had gotten almost the whole class playing soccer.

I was too proud to play

They were the captains and they would shout orders at their teammates.

Pass! Pass!

Tackle him and run at the goal!

They yelled, and the others obeyed them.

I watched how it worked

Sometimes the ball would come toward me.

Here!

Pass it!

I kicked it as hard as I could at the goal.

HNNF!

I really wished I could score a goal

Recess went on forever...

I said pass!

Pass it!

I became friendly with Brendan, a younger kid who didn't play soccer because he was afraid of the ball.

Wanna pass the ball to each other?

Yeah!

You and me are the same: we don't have a dad!

HUH? I have a dad!

Oh, really? I've never seen him!

He's a VERY important professor. He works in Saudi Arabia!

Ha ha ha, that's not a real country!

I never argued with Brendan. He was so sure of himself that it was impossible to change his mind.

I know all the countries in the world and there's no country with that name! Why lie?

Well, my father said it was real!

Well, he's wrong. Tell him I said so.

My mother made friends with Brendan's mother.

Ah! They're getting along well, that's nice!

Yes, Brendan is very mature for his age.

Exactly the same

Brendan, would you like to come play with Riad on Wednesday?

Yeah!

32

He started coming to our house every Wednesday. The same thing always happened.

At first we'd play together and everything would be fine.

Let's make the airplane fly!

It's not a plane, it's a space shuttle!

No, it's a plane! I know all about planes! You think you're so smart, Riad, but you're just a big fat show-off!

After that we'd play without talking to each other.

Here's the plane!

Whooosh!

Then he would end up playing with my brother.

Let's go over here. We don't need him!

I was left alone. I pretended not to care.

And the Challenger space shuttle is taking off. What a beautiful ... oh my God, it exploded! BLARGH!

Let's play hide and seek!

Yeah!

Actually very upset

The astronauts are burned alive. They die in agonizing pain.

Play wif me? Huh? We play? Huh?

We make da space shuddle fly?

HEY! GO AWAY!

Time passed slowly in Cap Fréhel.

Sometimes I'd go out alone to explore the land around our house.

Don't go far. And come back in 30 minutes, okay?

Okay!

I was worried I'd bump into a gang of enemy children, like I had in Ter Maaleh.

I made a weapon to defend myself

Twisted old stick

Rusty nail

Smell of wet grass

I walked down the path and came to a newly paved road.

Perfectly painted white lines

The few cars on the road swerved to avoid me.

I never saw anybody.

I looked through windows.

Children played inside houses. There was nobody outside.

After a while I ended up on a moor. The vegetation was low and thick.

I couldn't see it, but I could definitely smell the sea

Watching the waves break, I imagined terrible things.

So I decided ← to go home

I didn't miss my father but I often thought about him. I wondered what he was doing at that moment in Saudi Arabia...

How had he found a house there?

Where was he living? What if he was homeless and too scared to tell us?

What was he eating? He didn't even know how to boil an egg!

How did he wash his clothes? Or iron his shirts?

And what would happen if he lost his house keys and was locked inside?

Did he miss us?

What if he was run over by a bus? Who would tell us?

This guy has no family. Throw him in the dump.

What if he stole something because it was so tempting?

What if he was wrongly accused of murder?

Or maybe he'd made friends with the king of Saudi Arabia and forgotten all about us.

Whoa, this Porsche really goes fast!

ROAAR

In the supermarkets where my mother bought groceries, there were so many things to buy. But we often ate the same food.

Who wants this galette?

Me!!!

It was a sort of savory pancake that she browned in a pan. She broke an egg on top of it...

Warm, comforting smell

...then she added grated cheese and a slice of ham and folded the galette in two.

One of the most delicious meals in the world

I could eat it every day

Crunchy and chewy at the same time

Rich and delicately salted flavor

Mesmerizing

And for dessert we had Petit Suisse.

Petit-Suisse

A bit like Syrian labne, but sweeter and softer

Fantastic artificial smells of fruit

Sold in little multicolored containers

We were allowed only one each—except for Fadi, who had three.

That's all he eats, poor thing!

Wildly envious

When night fell, everybody went to bed.

We had no friends or acquaintances, and nobody ever visited us...

But one evening...

Tap Tap Tap

Somebody was walking on the gravel outside the house!!! Or was it the rain?

The leopard seal is the most fearsome predator in the Antarctic...

BANG BANG BANG!!!

WHO'S THERE?

Guess!

SURPRIIIIISE!

Mama! Who dat?

What do you mean, who's that?

Who's that?!

He doesn't recognize me! My own son!

See? I shaved my mustache because I know you hate it!

Why didn't you tell us you were coming?

I wanted it to be a surprise! I asked your mother where you live! I told her not to breathe a word, and obviously she didn't! Hee hee!

But are you back for good?

The Saudi school year is over for me. I don't have any more classes.

I wanted to come back for Riad's birthday.

So this is our French house!

Not bad!

Watch out, you're dripping!

But not very luxurious.

40

He inspected all the rooms.

Another floor! Wow!

He looked tired, and I could tell that he was pretending to be in a good mood.

Ah! The bathroom!

Very small shower.

Hardly even a shower at all, in fact...

Just a trickle.

What is this thing in Riad's room?

What thing?

The ceiling! It slopes!

Well, it's the roof!

Well, it's very, very sloping.

Look, I'm too tall.

You really don't notice anything, do you?

?

MY DIAMOND WATCH! LOOK!

I had never seen anything like it. It sparkled!

IS IT GENUINE?

OF COURSE!

I'll have to get it appraised. It was given to me by a member of the Saudi royal family!

HUH?!

I'll tell you all about it. But first, I need food.

I'M STARVING!

So it was true! He really had made his fortune!

See? Papa is rich now!

He ate as if he hadn't seen food in weeks

CRUNCH CRUNCH

He still chewed with his mouth open

CHOMP CHOMP CHOMP

42

Comfortable couch! I don't really like the green velvet though.

SCRATCH SCRATCH

CLICK

Whut's ull this crap on the TV?

Where am I supposed to put my lucky bull?

It's my collection of Kinder toys.

OK, then.

Aaah... Home at last!

CLICK CLACK

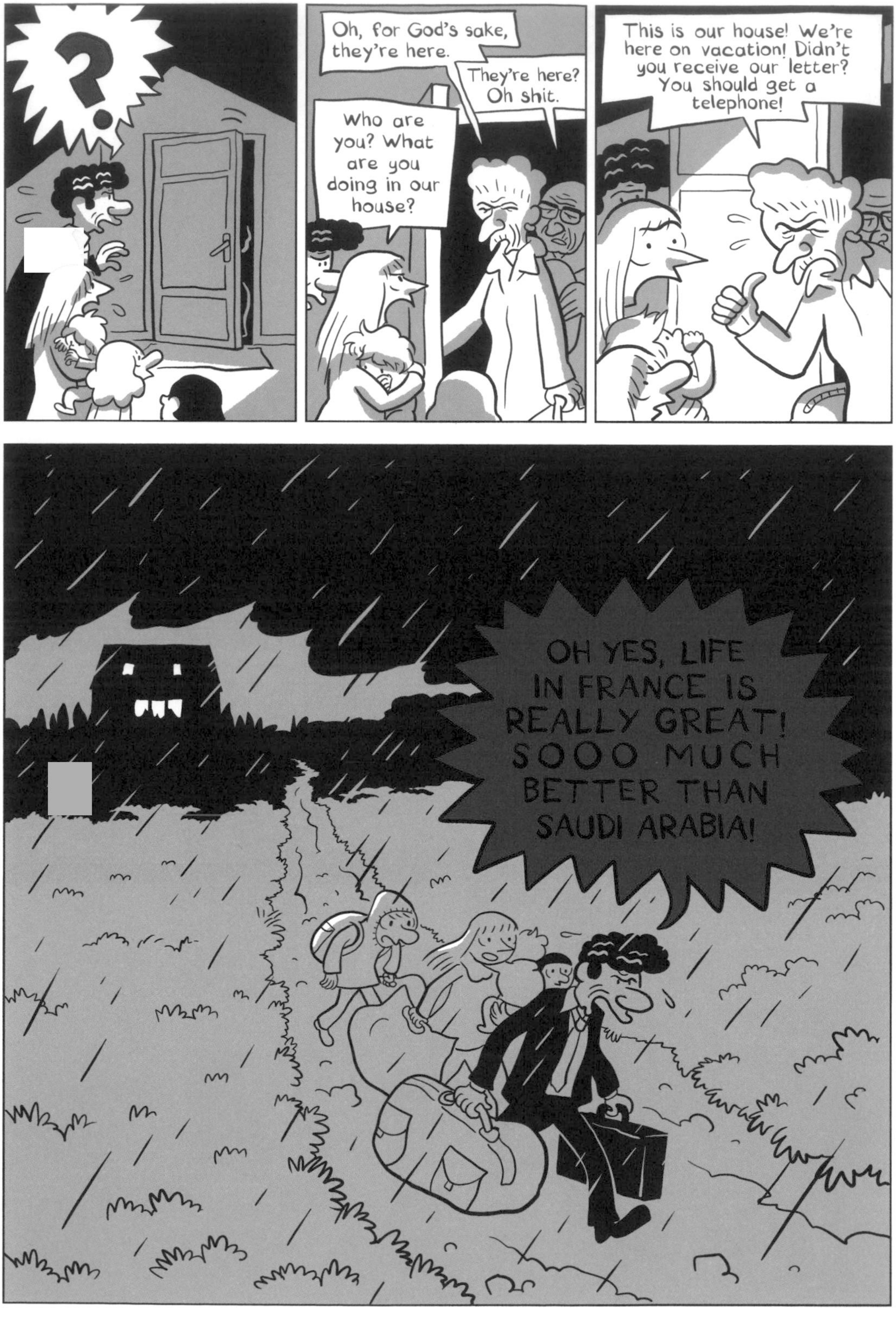
?
Oh, for God's sake, they're here.
They're here? Oh shit.
Who are you? What are you doing in our house?
This is our house! We're here on vacation! Didn't you receive our letter? You should get a telephone!
OH YES, LIFE IN FRANCE IS REALLY GREAT! SOOO MUCH BETTER THAN SAUDI ARABIA!

CHAPTER 2

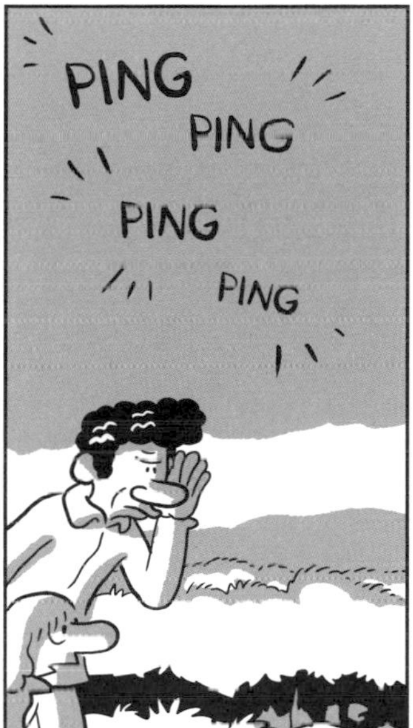
PING
PING
PING
PING

One of my students is a prince. A real prince. One day he comes to me at the end of class...

Doctor! Your class is fascinating. I would like to invite you to a small party this Friday, after the mosque, if you're free?

Oh! Um... I...

It would be my pleasure, Your Highness!

On Friday I took a cab there. The driver was a Filipino. Saudi Arabia is full of Filipinos. They're all slaves...

Is the palace much farther? I'm going to be late!

Me afraid of go there saidi!

The big wuss was crapping himself

Outside the building there was a military roadblock. The Filipino didn't want to go near it. I got out and he sped off.

HALT!

It was 120 degrees

The smaller of the two soldiers came up to me and told me to get lost. I didn't move. I looked him straight in the eye, that son of a dog!

I was invited by His Highness the prince. He's expecting me. I am Dr. Sattouf.

He took my papers, looked at them, looked at his list, called over the taller soldier, who also looked at them, then their expressions softened and they let me in.

I came to an entrance between marble pillars

Two Filipinos opened the door.

Hello saidi, me guide you to garden...

Very well...

Marble

47

Inside the palace, there was a real savanna! With tall grass and flat trees! It was incredible! It was Africa!

His Highness like Africa. He often go hunt there.

and some gazelles!

We walked for a long time, until we came to a tree. A rug was spread out in its shade. The prince and his guests were sitting on it.

Ah, doctor! Come quench your thirst...

A Filipino handed me a glass of orange juice. I sipped it. By God, it was the best orange juice I'd ever tasted!

I swear those oranges must have been grown in Paradise

The prince's dagger gleamed. It was pure gold, studded with precious stones.

I was looking at the prince when what did I see behind him? I swear it was real.

A giraffe...

and some gazelles!

So, I was drinking my delicious juice and wondering how anyone could have a giraffe and a herd of gazelles in their garden when suddenly the guests started shouting.

AAHH!

The king, AL ASSAD! AL ASSAD!

?

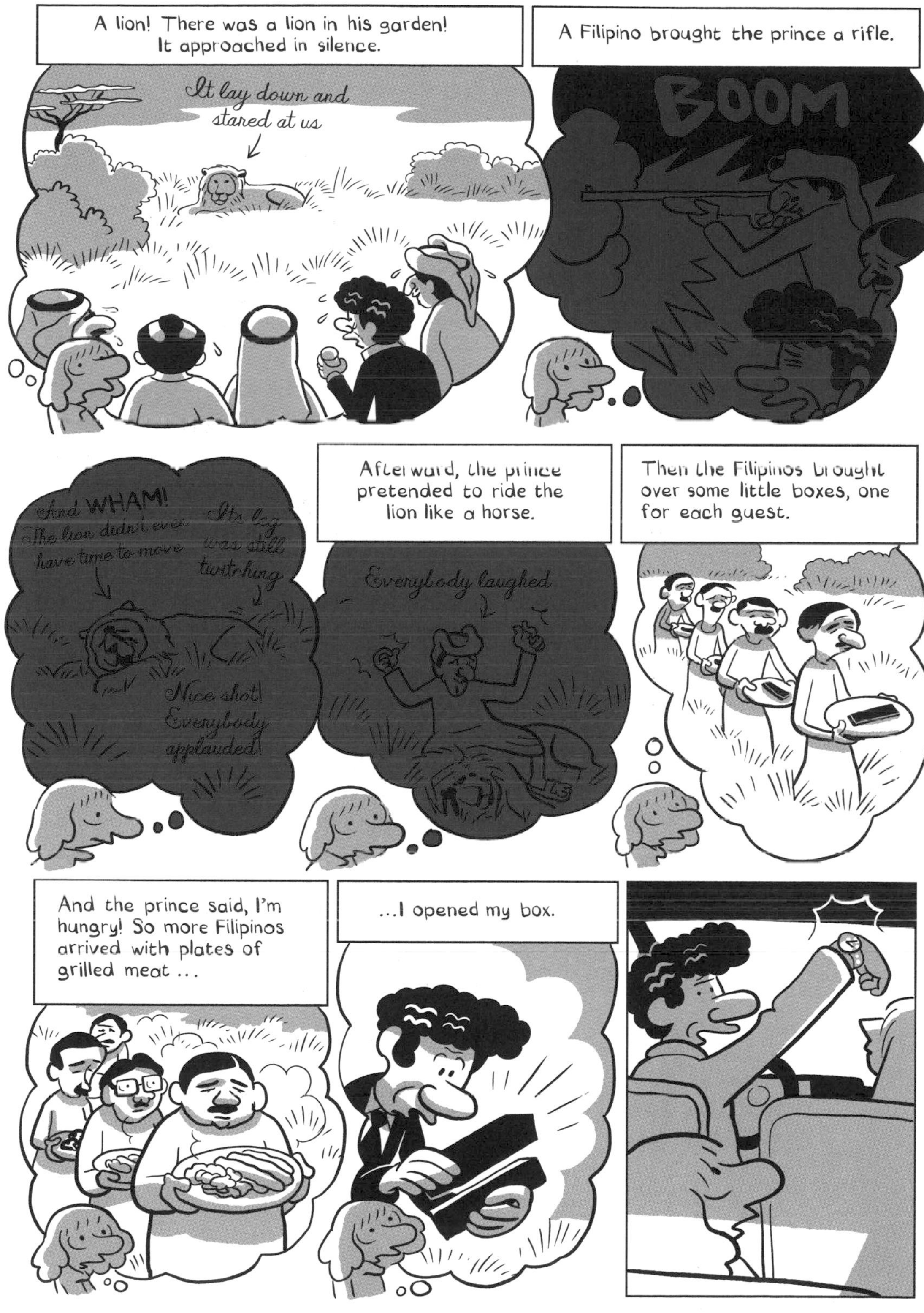
A lion! There was a lion in his garden! It approached in silence.
It lay down and stared at us
A Filipino brought the prince a rifle.
BOOM
And WHAM! The lion didn't even have time to move
Its leg was still twitching
Nice shot! Everybody applauded!
Afterward, the prince pretended to ride the lion like a horse.
Everybody laughed
Then the Filipinos brought over some little boxes, one for each guest.
And the prince said, I'm hungry! So more Filipinos arrived with plates of grilled meat . . .
. . . I opened my box.

I went back to my apartment and I stared at the watch all night.

All night!

A streetlamp sent a thin shaft of light through the window, and all the diamonds sparkled!

AAAAH! It's worth suffering alone there to see such beautiful things. ...

I feel sorry for the poor lion...

So, I tell you how hard I'm working and how lonely I am and all you care about is the lion? Ugh, that's the French for you! They prefer animals to people.

By the way, you really need to send me more money. We have three kids, you know...

You can't imagine how much they eat. They're like bottomless pits. Except for Fadi, who eats only Petit Suisse...

YOU MUST EAT LESS, CHILDREN! HOW DARE YOU EAT SO MUCH?!?

I know it's not easy, but since you didn't want to come to Saudi Arabia I've changed my strategy. I'm being careful with money, too, so I can save lots and send it to Jersey...

WHAT ABOUT US?

I've got an excellent high-interest account there, where the large sums I'm depositing grow and grow.

Money breeds money...

BUT WHAT ABOUT US? We need that money now!

We're using my grandparents' car

...and eventually there'll be so much that we can live on the interest alone!

We're so close!

After that, we'll be people of independent means. We won't have to work!

BUT WHEN? WHEN? WHEN?

I'M NOT GOING TO WAIT FOREVER, YOU KNOW! I've started looking for a job, by the way!

PFFFFT

Magnificent!

TABAC PRESSE
16 BIJOUTERIE

Really, this is beautiful work!

I've never seen a watch like this before.

The silver has been sculpted to perfection... All by hand, of course. I can offer you 4000 francs for it!

?

Only 4000 francs? With all these diamonds?

There are no diamonds. This is a silver watch.

WHAT? But... GRRRR!

Thank you.

Did you really think it was a diamond watch?

I could see in his eyes he was glad there were no diamonds!

JEWELER MY ASS!

RACIST! FILTHY FRENCH RACIST!

Citroën Visa...
What a crappy car!

Well, we're very grateful to Charles and Mama for lending it to us!

It'd be nice if we could buy a car, now that we're living in France...

Well, yeah, that's the plan: a good family sedan.

Really?

I'm still deciding between a BMW and a Mercedes...

It'll definitely be German anyway...

I'm so happy you're saying this!

I love the Germans.

My father kept yanking the steering wheel to the side.

When another car came toward us he yanked even harder, as if he were afraid we'd crash...

Mama's house is over there!

Hang on. I want to drop by our future house...

We drove all the way to the coast, near Cap Fréhel. Very few people lived there.

There was only one house →

This is the future Sattouf castle!

Whoa ... It's amazing ... but it's not for sale ...

This kind of place is never for sale.

You just have to turn up with a suitcase full of dollars and say: "Here, your chateau is mine now."

Look, it's not even inhabited.

I bet its owners have forgotten all about it.

But if it were ours, it would have to be a holiday home! Because there's no university near here ...

Where would you work?

When we're people of independent means, I won't have to work. We'll live like lords!

Don't you understand anything?

In the meantime, what do we do about getting more money each month?

Ask your mother! She's lucky enough to have you living with her. She can pay!

But she's not my husband!

Riad! Do you want to see the gates of Hell?

Huh? YEAH!

Follow me!

This is a very dangerous place. Walk carefully in my footsteps!

Now look.

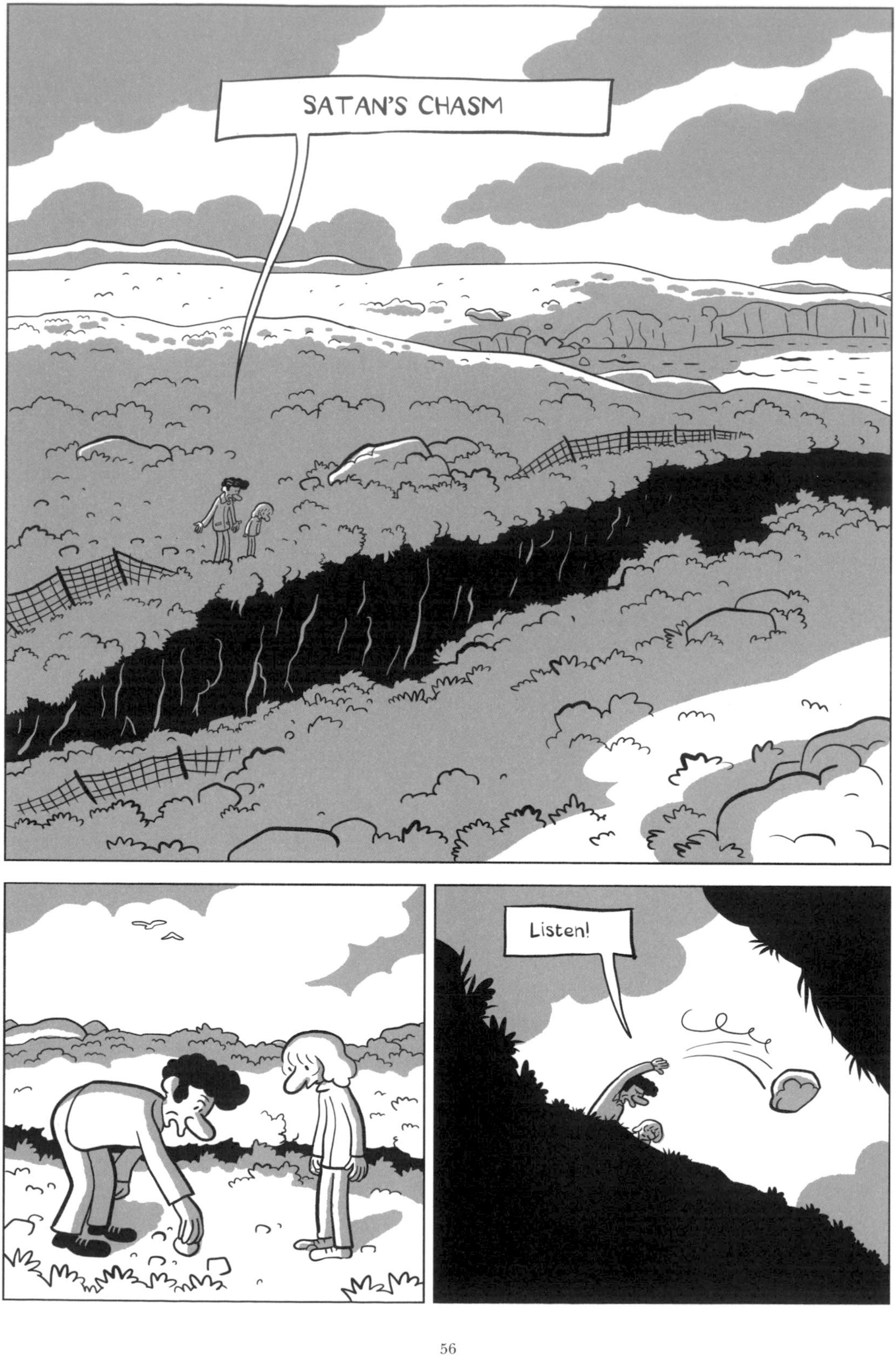
SATAN'S CHASM
Listen!

PING
PING
PING
PING

PING
PING
PING
PING -

PING
PING
PING

PING

Plop

Can you imagine how deep this thing is?

Did you hear how long it took for the stone to reach the bottom?

Scary, isn't it? Everything around us seems so normal, except for this deep, deep chasm right in front of us!

The village bell started ringing.

DONG!
DONG!
DONG!
DONG!
DONG!

Looks → worried

?

Watch out for the crevasse! Everybody around here knows about it.

Apparently it goes all the way under the church. Shall we go back? I have to feed the kids.

Satan!

The land of Satan!

DONG!
DING
DONG!

57

It was April 1988, and the French presidential elections were coming up. François Mitterrand was up for reelection.

I was not remotely interested in French politicians.

They were old, and I couldn't understand anything they said.

Lick it! Go on!

?

They could never agree on anything and were always putting on airs.

Come on, lick it, Moustik!

RIAD! WHAT THE HELL ARE YOU DOING?

WHY ARE YOU UNDER THE TABLE WITH THAT DISGUSTING DOG? COME HERE!

Don't touch it! It's dirty!

Moustik isn't dirty! He's just come back from the groomer!

So, Abdel, tell us about Saudi Arabia. How are things there?

Excellent, wonderful! It's a very wealthy country. Life there is much better than in France. Everyone is a millionaire.

Beautiful country.

I've heard there are terrible sandstorms in Riyadh.

I've never seen anything like that.

It's like the Côte d'Azur.

The weather is very good, very hot. Healthcare is free. We could easily live there and be very happy.

I adore Riyadh. Whenever I hear the name of that city, or read it on a sign, I think of my son!

And I feel less lonely...

Speaking of Riad, have you seen his drawings? He's so gifted!

Oh yeah?

Not bad. It's good to have a hobby!

It's more than that! I believe he'll be a great artist.

No, as I've said before, he will be a great doctor.

Look how well he draws shadows!

It's impossible to be an artist in France if you're an Arab.

Oh? Why's that?

Because of the Jews! They control everything—TV, books, music, politics.

I mean, how many Arabs do you see on TV? Paris is full of Arabs, but on TV, none at all!

Even an idiot can see that.

I think you're exaggerating . . .

Pffft. Turn on the TV now, and I bet we see a Jew!

Deal?

François Mitterrand appeared. He was being interviewed by the journalist Claude Sérillon.

YOU LOSE!

HA HA!

Pfft. How do you know he's not a Jew? It might just as easily have been Drucker or Elkabbach!

I never win the lottery, so it's hardly a surprise if I lose playing see the Jew on TV . . . But you French people know I'm right.

60

It's simple, Riad. The Jews have all the money. And because every family wants their money to stay in the family...

...no Jew will ever share his money with a non-Jew. Never mind an Arab!

Go ahead—try to be an artist. You'll see if your papa is right...

But why do they control everything?

Because of the Second World War.

Hitler, the German leader, went after the Jews. He killed lots of them! Because at the time the Jews had everything, shared nothing, and were hated by everybody.

Anyway, after the war, the Jews exaggerated Hitler's massacres so that everybody would feel sorry for them. Then they took control of the media to stop people from saying bad things about them.

But why?

BECAUSE OF ISRAEL OF COURSE! THEY TOLD **LIES** ABOUT CONCENTRATION CAMPS SO THEY COULD CREATE ISRAEL AND NOBODY COULD CRITICIZE IT!

And the Arabs get the worst of it, as always!

GOD, YOU'RE EVEN WORSE THAN YOU WERE BEFORE!

How can you say things like that in front of the children? It's disgusting!

DISGUSTING? IT'S HISTORY! I'M A DOCTOR OF HISTORY! I'M THE ONE WHO KNOWS STUFF! YOU DONT KNOW ANYTHING! I'M A DOCTOR! A WORLD-RENOWNED DOCTOR!

Whether you like it or not, the official history of France is controlled by the Jews so they can protect Israel. That's not my fault!

But one day, history will be overturned! The Arabs will have their revenge, and Israel and its allies will be defeated.

We lived through the Second World War. And I can tell you one thing: the Krauts were bastards. All of them!

When I worked for the Post Office during the occupation, there were Germans there, too. German women. And they were horrible. They pushed us down the stairs...

The gray mice, we called them.

They really thought they were superior to us. They were just bad people. RACISTS! Evil, pure and simple.

And that's not official history telling you that, it's me! ME! I saw it with my own eyes! YOU SAW NOTHING!

Sniff

I was kidding! Ha ha ha! Can't you people take a joke?

The Jews don't control everything.

That's exaggeration.

Most of them are nice, normal people, like you and me.

When I went to Morocco, it was a Jew who helped me settle in.

And I'm not Jewish.

I wanted to open a little photography store in Mogador, but no bank would lend me the money. Somebody told me about a man who would give me credit. A Jew.

He lent me the money, and I paid him back. It was thanks to him that I could open my store.

See, for once it wasn't me saying that the Jews have all the money!

It wasn't me!

And I'll see you next Sunday, at seven o'clock, for another edition of 7Sur7...

...when we will of course be discussing the reelection of François Mitterrand...

Look at her! That's Anne Sinclair, a journalist!

Pfft.

She has one of the most popular shows on TV. And she's a Jew, obviously.

Look how she pretends that everything is okay. She talks about lots of subjects on the show, but you'll never hear her say anything bad about Israel.

She never mentions that the Arabs are suffering. She acts as if they don't exist, as if they're not being killed... and the French believe her. THAT'S the Jews for you!

They twist things.

One day, you'll realize that Papa was right. You'll see.

Yes, Papa.

Ah ben shela wahala... Hasha wo...

Hasha wo

I couldn't understand what he was muttering.

He was staring into space

Na ma wulah

CHAPTER 3

We went back to Syria a few weeks later.

My Syrian grandmother had a bad case of pneumonia. She didn't have long to live.

CREAK
CREAK

PING

CREAK

I had to leave fourth grade before the end of the year. My mother had agreed to make the trip one last time.

I need to change Fadi's diaper!

WE DON'T HAVE TIME! Someone will steal our luggage!

I had forgotten how long and complicated the journey to Syria was.

THAT'S OUR BAG! STOP!

HAII SHENTAITI RAJILI SHENTAITI!

She was casually walking away with our bag

There were so many obstacles, problems, noises, crowds...

What's the soldier saying?

I don't know! I don't understand anything!

Mak basse hek masari? Ma bikafi, atini dollarat kaman!

Ma ma'air ghir hedul.

La tetesele ya said, lakeele shoyaet dollarat!

...France seemed so calm in comparison.

Men stared strangely at my mother.

My father wanted to take a minibus because it was cheaper...

...but he ended up paying for a cab and sulking about it.

The little gray houses flashed past the windows.

We drove past abandoned building sites...

The car ride went on forever...

Then we came within sight of Homs and Ter Maaleh, where there was a power outage.

The house was freezing. My father fired up the generator and then lit the oil stove.

BRRRR

Both worked.

What's that?

It's pretty. It's a print of Degas's painting of a dancer... to hide the cracks and the blank wall.

My toys were still there.

They were covered in dust and smelled musty

Fadi slept in my parents' bedroom, Yahya and I in our old beds.

GOD IS GREAT AND THERE IS NONE GREATER ... THAN GOD! CREAK!

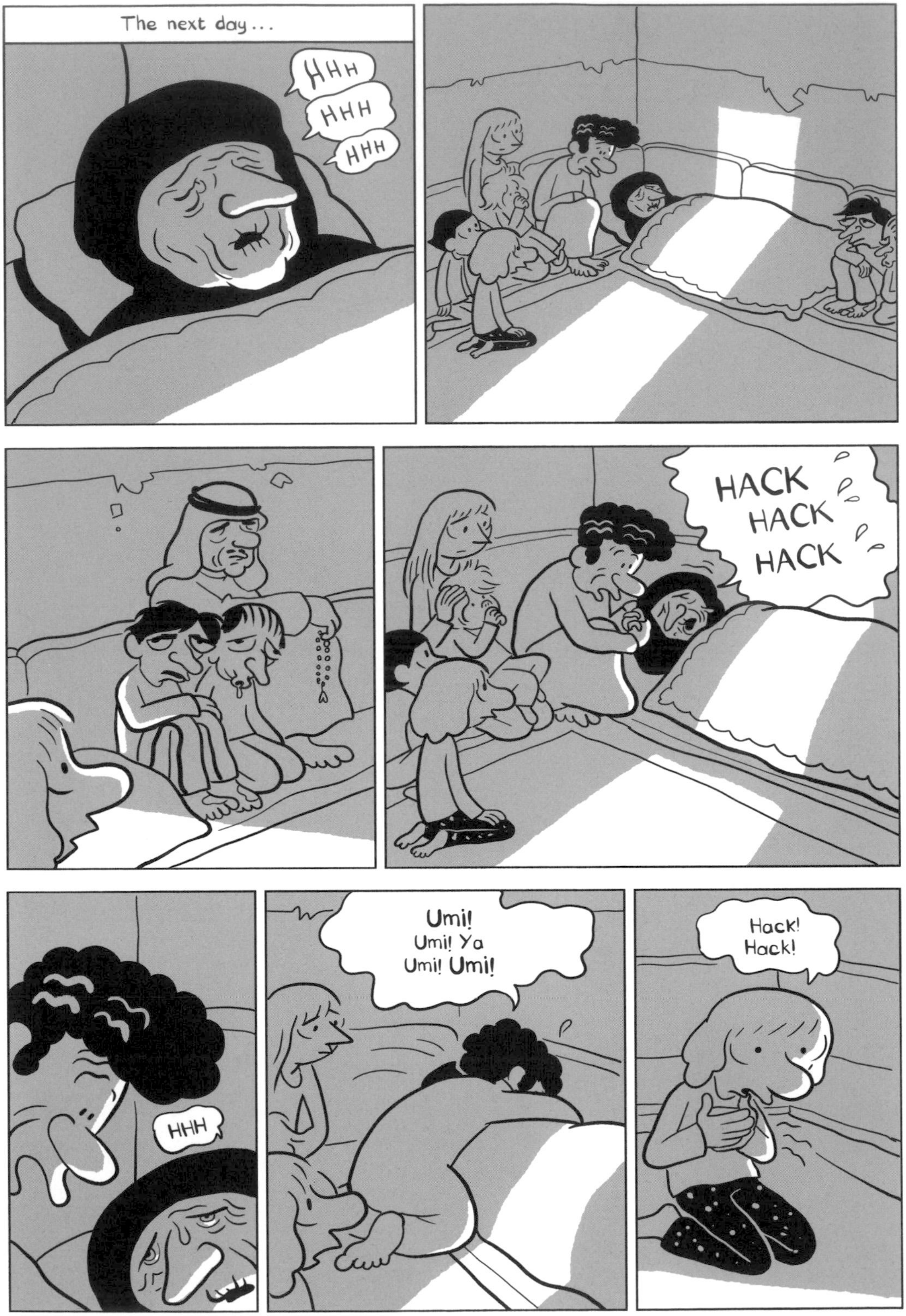

The next day...
HHH
HHH
HHH
HACK
HACK
HACK
HHH
Umi!
Umi! Ya
Umi! Umi!
Hack!
Hack!

My father found some antibiotics, and my grandmother soon got better.

She looked perfectly fine

Life went on in the gray house.

The apartment had not changed.

The only new thing was my mother's picture

The cracks in the walls were so bad we could see the outside from the kitchen.

My mother homeschooled me.

Show me the complement of the direct object.

There.

That's right.

Pure boredom

Because I no longer spoke Arabic, I couldn't go to the village school.

Happiest kid in the world

You already know that. And that...

I can't believe we're stuck in this hole again...

71

Your mother is better now. I want to go back to France.

Huh? And what if she dies in the next few weeks?

She's over the illness, but she's still very tired...

Riad needs to go to school!

I agree. I'll enroll him next week.

IN FRANCE! NOT HERE!

There's no point. The school year is almost over. We can spend the summer here, and you'll go back to France for the start of fifth grade.

And you?

Me? I'll go back to teaching in Saudi Arabia... ALONE...

POOR ME...

WHY DON'T YOU JUST LOOK FOR A JOB IN FRANCE INSTEAD OF WHINING?!

I'm kidding...

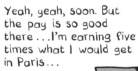

Yeah, yeah, soon. But the pay is so good there...I'm earning five times what I would get in Paris...

When I've saved enough we'll move to France, if God wishes it.

NOT IF GOD WISHES IT. I WISH IT!

HA! SHE THINKS SHE'S GOD NOW!

French women really have a high opinion of themselves!

HEE HEE HEE! IT'S A JOKE!

You're right. Don't worry.

Here, I got you a present. I found a copy of *Paris Match* in Homs!

My father radiated happiness at being back in his village.

Ahlan wa sahlan...

Ahlan wa sahlan...

We went for a walk near his land...

...and my mother discovered that he'd been hiding things from her.

A brick wall had been built around his field.

WHAT THE HELL IS THAT?

It's a wall to protect our fruit trees from the village kids!

You never mentioned this to me! And why is it missing a side?

Oh, four sides would have been too expensive. I'll do the other one next year.

Four big holes had been dug.

And this? What's this?

Well, it's um... the foundations for our villa...

But you said you were saving the money so we could move to France. You said you'd look for a job in Paris!!!

Well, yeah, but what if I don't find anything?

Anyway, we can have both—a beautiful villa here and a house in France...

I'm earning so much money in Saudi Arabia.

I don't even know how much you earn!

You give me 2500 francs a month...

Come and live in Saudi Arabia with me. I'll tell you everything...

Instead of leaving me alone like a dog.

My mother went back to the apartment to look after my brothers. I stayed with my father.

The bricks in the wall were already full of holes. They crumbled when I touched them.

Don't put your hands there! There could be snakes in the holes!

Look, Riad. I'm going to show you something I did for you.

Because you are my eldest son.

I planted a berry tree for you!

This is yours!

You remember when we ate berries together in Libya, when you were a little boy? I used to throw sticks into the tree to make the fruit fall...

Yes!

Ah, good times...

You and me, we're the same. Berries are our favorite fruit. Look at that tree! I only just planted it, but it's growing so fast. It feels at home here, on its land.

JUST LIKE US!

Wouldn't you like us to live here, in a beautiful palace?

Well, um...

On your ancestors' land?

I dunno, I...

Riad! You have to take your father's side! You are a MAN now!

Your mother can't imagine how happy we'll be in this house. France! France! It's all she talks about!

She has no vision. She's a woman...

76

You must think like me! We're Muslims, and good Muslim boys follow their fathers and listen to them.

It's the men who decide!

Look at this pile of bricks that the builders left.

Come on!

OOOOOH!

OOOOOH!

OOOOOH!

TAP
TAP

I'm doing that to scare off the snakes. They hate loud noises.

They've all gone now.

There are HUFF two kinds of snakes here HUFF

The small ones, which are highly poisonous and dangerous ...

HUFF

HUFF!

And the big black ones

HUFF!

Scary but harmless.

HUFF!

HE WAS BUILDING A SORT OF HUT!

I don't like — HUFF — either of them.

HUFF
HUFF

THUMP

I thought the hut he'd built was magnificent.

This is the first version of our luxury house.

LET'S GO IN.

We lay on the ground side by side.

PHEW! PHEW! PHEW!

I listened to my father breathing, to the wind rustling the leaves in the trees.

Smell of dry grass

Riad! I have to tell you what I did in Saudi Arabia.

One day I took a bus with two colleagues from the university, an Egyptian and a Saudi, and we made the pilgrimage to Mecca.

Everybody was excited and emotional. I was very young when my mother took me there, so in a way it was like my first time.

I live in Saudi Arabia and I'm going to Mecca, by God!

My life is a success.

When we arrived, it was wonderful—we put big white sheets over our bodies and walked seven times around the black stone.

Never in my life had I seen anything so beautiful. We moved closer, and I saw the place where you can TOUCH the stone.

Almost everybody there was trying to touch it. A mass of people, all shoving forward... I was almost within reach when an old man pushed in front of me!

He had no hand →

AND THEN THE FILTHY LEPER TOUCHED THE STONE WITH HIS STUMP!

So I didn't touch the stone. I turned around and left. I didn't want to go after him...It's silly, but diseases disgust me...

Afterward, I regretted it so much! I blamed that poor leper for spoiling my moment... but, well, it's important to be merciful and not have bad thoughts about the poor.

I prayed and prayed, and I remembered when I'd come with my mother and lost her in the crowd...and then found her again, thanks be to God.

What power I felt

I thought back to all those years of my life that had been lived in vain, all that time wasted, all that time spent so far from religion...

I regretted not having made the pilgrimage before.

All that marble, those lights, that magnificent beauty...I was overwhelmed.

I wept with emotion, because I'm very sensitive.

The Egyptian guy was sobbing like a baby from all the emotion

I hadn't booked a hotel room (too expensive), so we slept in the camp at Mina, a place with thousands of tents for pilgrims—and it's free.

My God, it was hot →

Well, every year there are fires and deaths in the camp, so first I walked around and checked where all the exits were.

Hm. The desert is on this side.

When we went to Mount Ararat, there was such a huge crowd, it was scary. It was total chaos.

I was crushed, I couldn't breathe

Thankfully there was an army helicopter flying very low over the crowd to frighten people and herd them in the right direction.

WRRRR

← Very smart

All the believers in the world were there, equal before God, side by side ...

The stumpy ... and the rich

You're not allowed to wear any clothing with stitching on it there, just a white sheet, and you have to shave your head or cut your hair.

I cut it just a bit.

Afterward you have to gather seven stones from the ground and throw them at the pillars that represent the Devil.

We were going to stone Satan

You get hit by the stones of the people next to you and behind you (thankfully they were very small stones).

My Egyptian colleague went crazy—he went into a trance or something. When he'd run out of stones, he threw his shoe at the pillar!

YAH!

HA HA! HOW WE LAUGHED AT THAT EGYPTIAN GUY!

He was a nutcase!

Hey, look. I asked my Saudi colleague to take a picture of me that day.

I always keep it with me.

This is me with the Devil.

The wind began to blow. The bricks moved a little bit, so we left the hut.

He cleaned the ground, then rubbed earth against his ankles and wrists.

GOD IS GREEEEEEEAAAAAAAT!

Now I can call myself Hadj! Hadj Abdel!

God is great...

It was the first time I'd ever seen my father pray.

I'd completely forgotten my Arabic. I couldn't understand anything now.

Shlonak ya Riad?

It was like the language had run away while I'd turned my back.

Heeee

Yet when people spoke Arabic in front of me, something inside my head moved.

The sounds were rich and mysteriously beautiful.

Sharo ma aad ashkar! Heeee!

I was mesmerized...

Hala shaar louno benii!

I felt as if part of me were awakening.

SMACK!

My father went to fetch my cousins Wael and Mohamed so they could play with me.

They'd grown

They were very nice and polite, but something in their attitude had changed.

CRASHHH!

Their expressions were very serious. They looked at me solemnly.

I felt inferior.

They were little men

I was a baby

GOD IS GREAT AND NOTHING IS GREATER THAN GOD...

When the call to prayer sounded, they threw the toys aside...

...and ran home to pray with their family.

They came back looking worried about me.

I felt embarrassed, inconsequential...

They seemed to pity me

Crushed by their moral superiority.

When was I going to start believing in God?

Cough cough

Since I didn't go to school, my father would take me for walks in the village, hoping it would help bring back my Arabic.

One day, we saw a tractor driven by a young, blond, European-looking man.

Look, it's Ahmad and Abu Ahmad!

Ahmad spoke perfect Arabic, with no accent.

Salaam ya Hadj!

Abu Ahmad is my cousin—he was in the army—and Ahmad, the blond guy, is his son from his marriage to a Russian woman.

They got married during his studies in the USSR

The woman's parents were scientists

Then, when his studies were over, Abu Ahmad decided to go back to Syria with his family to live on his land.

They arrived in Damascus and took a cab to Ter Maaleh. They were very happy... and suddenly Abu Ahmad saw the moon.

Svetlana, my darling! Look at the moon of my country. Look how beautiful it is.

CRASH!

It was so unlucky! The stupid cab driver looked at the moon, too, and didn't see the truck coming toward them!

Abu Hamad's poor Russian wife was killed instantly. He and his son were injured, but they survived.

Oh how sad!

His wife was buried in the village cemetery, and a little later he married a local peasant woman.

Now his tall blond son helps his father in the fields. He doesn't remember anything about his mother or the USSR.

He's a good Muslim. But what a sad story...

The moon! Look at the moon!

CRASH!

I asked my father how the Russian family reacted, and if they still saw one another.

No, never. He told them their daughter was dead, and he never saw them again.

The parents tried, but ...

It made Abu Ahmad too sad. It reminded him of his dead wife...

And the plane tickets to the USSR were so expensive! Can you imagine? It makes you sad AND costs you a fortune! What's the point?

Those walks with my father always ended the same way.

We sat with some men he had known when he was a boy. They drank tea outside their houses.

These men's attitude toward my father had changed.

My father spoke in a serious voice...

...and they listened.

I caught a few words. They were talking about plantings, harvests, about God, who decided all things and to whose will one must submit.

He was far more confident than before.

He gave the impression that he had finally become someone important.

For years my father had tried to earn the admiration of the other men in his village.

They were not interested in his PhD...

...his life in France...

...or his work in Damascus.

But living in Saudi Arabia and his pilgrimage to Mecca had changed everything.

GOD IS GREEEEAT AND THERE IS NONE GREEEEATER THAN GOD

He was now considered a very pious man and an example to others.

It was springtime in Ter Maaleh.

My father was teaching a few classes in Damascus. When he wasn't home, my mother grumbled all day long.

And now I'm alone again, the little housewife!

It's unbelievable!

Wah, Mamaaa

She talked to herself, prowling around like a caged animal.

What have I done to the Good Lord to deserve this?

It won't last. No way!

Mamaaa

In the evening, when my father came home, she didn't get up to say hello or kiss him.

Is your mother in the bedroom?

Yes

Thanks be to God.

So, apart from that, did everything go well at home today?

Um yeah.

Don't forget—you're the man of the house when I'm not around.

I could barely understand a word of spoken Arabic, but I could still read it pretty well.

Rhada Osama mina al madrassa.

Gooood!

You see? You haven't forgotten!

That's it, my son!

I didn't dare admit to my father that I had practically no idea what any of it meant.

Aheb madrashati

I was sure he must realize this even if he pretended not to.

Madrassati! Not madrashati!

He never asked me any questions about the meaning

Madrassati

That's it!

So one day he decided that I would go back to school.

No pressure! I'll understand if you're not top of the class.

Sniff

91

I had to go to school all day now. There was no cafeteria, so I took a packed lunch.

One of the few French foods that was easy to find in Homs and that children loved was Laughing Cow cheese.

I'm wrapping your sandwich in aluminum foil.

I know school isn't great here, but it's probably better for you to do something with your days, sweetie...

Next year, you'll go to school in France. I promise!

Stick with it!

My father walked me to school.

It still smelled of urine and pine trees

A wall had been built around the grounds

92

We walked through the courtyard.

The principal gave me books that he had put aside for me.

My father looked annoyed

Then we followed him down the hall.

I'm not happy. He wants to put you with the younger kids, that jerk!

He said you've been away for too long.

You need to catch up quickly, so you can get back to your class.

You're two years behind now.

It's shameful for a professor's son.

At that moment, we walked past one of my old teachers.

He hadn't changed

How was I going to be top of my class again when I didn't understand Arabic?

We came to a classroom. Three students were waiting outside.

Shu hada, ya kalb?

THWACK

The principal hit them as hard as he could. The sound of those thwacks echoed through the corridor like a drum.

Don't feel sorry for them—they're idiots.

BOOM!
BOOM
BOOM

→Unforgettable sound

After punishing them, he sent them back into the classroom...

I'm off! Have a good day!

...and then it was my turn.

Ahlan wa sahlan, ya Riad!

This young, dark-haired woman really was my teacher. She made me sit at the front.

Which just happened to be empty

She explained to the students that I came from France and asked if anybody knew where that country was. Some kids at the back began to mess around.

She asked them to stop, but they didn't. So she sent them outside.

I understood then that she refused to hit her students.

Yahudi!

I tried to follow the classes, but I understood nothing.

The teacher turned to question me sometimes.

Riad? Endak fikra?

Ma...Ana ma ba'aref...

"I don't know" in Arabic

Because she never hit anybody, the class was unruly.

When the students became too noisy or started fighting, she told them to leave.

That calmed them down a little. They were scared the principal would see them in the corridor and give them a thrashing.

At recess, I went to pee behind the school (there were still no toilets).

Toxac stink

I run away and tried to find an adult to hide behind.

I saw my old friend Saleem walk past.

Finally lunchtime arrived. I ate my Laughing Cow sandwich.

Despite his promises, my father no longer wanted to move to France.

But when I met you, you wanted to travel, to be independent...

Family is the most important thing! FA-MI-LY!

Now living in your village near your mother is your only dream!

Oh, like you don't want to live near your mother! That's why you want to live in France, to be close to her!

And I KNOW she's the one who told you not to go with me! She never liked me because she's a RACIST!

What are you talking about? You're crazy!

With all the money I earned in Saudi Arabia, we could live like kings here! We'd live in a beautiful villa, I'd hire private tutors for the children...

With a top education, they'd become rich, famous doctors, each with a different specialty.

Riad: a great neurosurgeon, because that's the hardest one.

Performing brain surgery ...

The medical elite.

GULP!

Yahya: pediatrician, to stop children dying at birth.

Okay, Papa!

And Fadi: oncologist, because cancer is the disease of the future.

?

My mother spent her days looking out her bedroom window, as if searching for a solution she couldn't find.

To make the time pass more quickly, I drew constantly.

Riad! Listen carefully to your papa. NEVER marry a Frenchwoman. They always want to do whatever they like. You should marry a SYRIAN woman!

They're just as beautiful and intelligent as Frenchwomen, but they will follow you EVERYWHERE and never complain.

THEY WILL OBEY YOU.

EVERYWHERE.

They'll follow you everywhere.

99

After a few weeks my Arabic finally came back to me... and a boy named Maher started doing this:

He'd had to repeat several grades

Sitting alone on his bench

He stared at me intensely all morning.

Looks ultraviolent →

No collar or hat ←

Bull neck →

Hair on his upper lip ←

At lunchtime he stood up and came to my table...

...opened my schoolbag, rummaged around inside...

...took out my Laughing Cow sandwich, and ate it.

Still smiling ↓

Aluminum foil folded by my mother

Bon appétit, darling!

The first time, I tried to stop him, but he was so strong I couldn't even move his arm.

Stop it, Jew, or I'll stab you in your belly.

← Shard of glass

The teacher pretended not to see anything.

One day, though, I told her about it.

Miss! Maher is eating my sandwich!

Ah um...I...What do you want me to do about it?

He's the principal's nephew...

I never said anything to my parents. I was scared that he would kill them, too.

I just didn't eat lunch anymore.

The older boys all had me down as a Jew.

At the end of the day, I ran from the school

Going home (which wasn't far away) was dangerous.

I had to assess the threat from the boys in my way before I got too close.

Let him come. I'll crack his skull...

NO ENTRY TO JEWS!

Some of them ran after me for no reason.

HUFF HUFF HUFF HUFF

Others threw stones at me.

Pure terror

The situation had gotten worse. I didn't know why.

Home! Only a few more yards...

One day, I understood.

Safe!

My cousins Anas and Moktar watched me pass by without saying anything

They had grown big and tough

That's the Jew! Why'd you let him go without beating him up?

Another time. We can't kill him in our nephew's building.

He's just come back from Israel. There'll be other opportunities.

Anas and Moktar had told the children in the village that I was Israeli. They all wanted to kill me.

Look at the village! There's no light!

The power's out! But here ...BRIGHT LIGHTS! What more do you want?

I'm not going to congratulate you because we have electricity! It's only here that you'd think that's a big deal!

I buy a generator. YOU'RE NOT HAPPY. I buy mineral water. YOU'RE NOT HAPPY. YOU'RE NEVER SATISFIED!

When we buy a chateau, you'll probably complain that the pool isn't big enough

FRENCHWOMEN! FRENCHWOMEN! MY GOD!

I'm going next door!

The door to Wael and Mohamed's apartment was always open.

Everyone took off their shoes before going in. Except me.

They'd never said anything about it

104

My cousins were doing their homework next to an oil lamp (they didn't have a generator).

They were very serious. I waited in silence for them to finish.

Their mother was pregnant, again.

I'm done!

Me too!

Nobody paid much attention to her

Their father was exhausted by his job as a middle school teacher. He lay there, gazing at his children.

He looked happy and calm

Wael and Mohamed were model students...

Shall we play cards, by God?

...but they were nothing compared to their big sister Qumar, who had a 100 percent average.

A game of shaddeh?

Yes, by God.

Shaddeh is the Arabic name for Kemps. You play it in teams of two. Each team agrees on a secret signal for when one of the players has four matching cards.

Qamar, do you want to play when you're done?

Coming!

You want to be on my team, Riad?

The game ends when the signal has been sent and the team wins a point. But if the other team spots the secret signal, they call out "counter Shaddeh" and they win the point.

Let's make a sign to fool them. I'll ask you if you have lots of toys in France...

They'll think that's our secret signal and call us out. And we'll win, ha ha.

Qamar was unbeatable.

Do you have lots of toys in France, Riad?

Counter Shad—

SHHH!

They're faking!

Yes, lots of toys...

Um...

My cousins were obsessed by the immorality of French people.

Do the French pray five times a day?

Well, um... No...they're not Muslims...

In my grandmother's village, there are only Christians...

...and ATHEISTS who don't believe in ANY God!

ARGH! How horrible!

But are there really no Muslims in France?

I've never seen any, but I think there are some in Paris.

They relaxed when they heard that.

Aah! What a difficult mission! They have to convert all those infidels...

But, thanks be to God, the French will all become good Muslims soon.

And when France is Muslim, if the Christians want to remain Christian, they'll be able to, because Muslims are very tolerant. They'll just have to pay a tax to the Muslims.

But, between us, that's idiotic. Paying to remain an infidel! Paying to go to Hell!

Is it really ONLY Muslims who go to Heaven?

OF COURSE! WHAT A QUESTION!

ALL INFIDELS WILL GO TO HELL!

Be careful, Riad.

But it's God who decides.

Have you ever met any Jews?

No!

But there are Jews in the streets of France, aren't there?

I don't know, but I've seen them on TV.

How can anyone live in a country where Jews appear on TV as if it's normal?!

And you, Riad? By God, are you spreading the good word to your French grandparents?

Have you told them they must convert if they want to go to Heaven?

You must help them!

Um well...

And you? You don't pray, by God! When are you going to start?

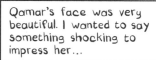

My father said I can wait until next year...

Hmm.

Qamar's face was very beautiful. I wanted to say something shocking to impress her...

...so I started saying anything that came into my head.

Did you know that my French grandparents have a ghost in their house? And they're friends with it!

AGH!

You can't see it, but the couch moves, and then you know it's sitting down.

And then you hear it chewing.

Eeeeeek!

How pretty she was when she was scared.

Riad, ghosts and genies are the soldiers of SATAN!

But this ghost is really nice! He never hurts anybody... He's no friend of the Devil...

Sometimes he even helps clear the table.

The plates fly into the kitchen...

Maybe it's a strange kind of ghost... Are you SURE your grandmother isn't Jewish?

Of course.

SHADDEH!

We win!

I often asked my father to tell me about his life in Saudi Arabia.

In Riyadh, I live in a small apartment, very modern. There's an elevator in the building (a modern luxury machine that means you don't have to climb the stairs).

Outside it's 110 degrees

I smoke Dunhills while I prepare my lectures, but I'm sometimes a little cold at home because the air-conditioning is not adjustable.

I sleep, and then in the morning I wake up and drink some very hot tea, and then I put on my suit and tie.

I carry my briefcase along the sidewalk to the University of King Saud. It's very hot, and I try to hurry because the suit makes me sweat.

To amuse myself, I count luxury cars

Six Mercedes W126s already! Wow!

When I get to the university, I go to my classroom, where my students are waiting for me. I teach the class and then I go home and tell myself: another $150 earned (I've calculated how much I earn every day).

So that's what I do with my days.

And I miss my children.

Do you teach girls as well as boys?

Of course! But the girls are on a different day, and I'm not allowed to see them, obviously.

The girls come one day a week. I never pass them in the corridors. I don't even know which door they use to enter the university.

TAP TAP
TAP

The university is empty on the girls' day

I have to go into a small windowless room. There's a camera, a table, and a chair.

Comfortable calfskin leather.

The camera transmits the image to a TV screen in a room where the women are. They can see me, but I can't see them because that's indecent and forbidden by religion.

But Brezhnev courageously refused to be intimidated by the United States and . . .

When the light goes out that means the class is over and I can go home.

Another $150 in my pocket!

I wonder how many Mercedes I'll see on the way home!

God, it's all so depressing! How can you bear to live in a country with laws and customs like that?

Life is easy there, if you're rich. You have a house, a garden...It's an Islamic country that scrupulously follows the religious laws. You judge it harshly because you know nothing about it.

It's a very pious country.

I have learned to love it.

The school principal and my father decided that my knowledge of the Quran was not good enough.

The Arabic in the Quran was not the same as the Arabic spoken in class

I had to spend every recess doing extra classes with my teacher.

Go on, Riad!

This was fine with me, because everybody wanted to kill me at recess

Tell me what this verse is about.

I couldn't tell if she was serious or just pretending. I could barely read it.

I...I don't know...

YAWNNN

All right, never mind. Let's start again. Listen...

She smelled of soap and, beneath that, the comforting, intoxicating scent of her sweat.

Bismillah a-rahman a-rahim

I enjoyed listening to her

After three or four "I don't know's," she burst out laughing.

HA HA this is completely pointless isn't it?

HA HA!

I wished recess could go on forever.

Her hand was warm

There's something I'm wondering: if you're French, why do you live here, not in France? France is much better!

I wish I could live there...

Paris!

It's because my father is Syrian. So I have to live here because I'm Syrian like him, and Syria is my country.

Hmm...

Did you come from France on a plane?

Yeah. I love flying on a plane. Do you like that too, Miss?

HA HA! There's no plane between Homs and Ter Maaleh!

All right. Shall we try reading again?

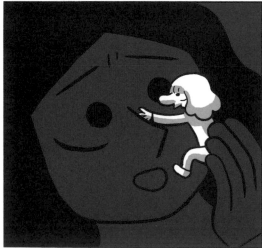

I dreamed about her every night.

One morning a few weeks later, my father came into my bedroom.

Don't wake your brother. Come with me!

It was the school holidays

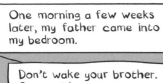

He was leaving to teach in Damascus.

I'm going to give you an important mission today!

It's important, but you mustn't worry.

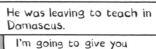

I haven't spoken to your mother about it. I'm talking to you because you're the eldest.

Today, somebody might knock at the door. You must not open it.

Even if it's your friends, or if a voice tells you to open up, don't.

A VOICE?

You stop moving and you wait for the people to leave.

What people?

YOU MUST NOT OPEN THE DOOR.

That's all.

Understood?

Yes.

And if your mother tries to open it, stop her. I'm off to Damascus!

See you later.

I waited all morning.

What monster might come?

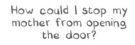

How could I stop my mother from opening the door?

Thankfully, she locked herself in her bedroom with my brothers and played with them.

BOOM! BOOM! BOOM!

?!? ?!?

Boom Boom Boom

BOOM BOOM BOOM BOOM!

116

Luckily, my mother and my brothers were asleep.

CLICK

After a while I heard footsteps on the stairs.

They were moving away

It was the first time I'd ever seen police in Ter Maaleh.

They ended up leaving

What did they want with my father?

Was someone at the door?

Um, no I don't know...

Oh, I thought...

Ah well, who cares? We never have any visitors in this hole...

Hellooo!

Papa!

The um... police... came here...

But I didn't open the door!

My father's face froze.

Uh, it's not a big deal...

They won't come back...

What did they want?

It's complicated... They didn't want anything... These police—they don't know what they're doing...

Don't worry about it.

Just don't mention it to your mother.

Don't mention what to me?

My father confessed that he had some problems.

It was no longer possible to stay in Syria

Good news!

At 30 he had moved to France to escape his mandatory military service.

Twenty years later, they'd caught up with him.

He'd paid bribes to lots of people who were supposed to declare him unfit for service.

Kissing while sniffing, which means we won't see each other for a long time

Smack!

But the only effect of the bribes had been to attract other people who also wanted bribes.

Holding back the tears

My father could no longer enter or leave Syria by plane. He was considered a deserter.

AIR FRA

We went back to France without him.

...We will be landing in Paris at 5:50 pm...

AIR FRANCE

My father was planning to leave Syria, too. He would travel to Saudi Arabia by car, passing through Jordan on his French passport.

CHAPTER 4

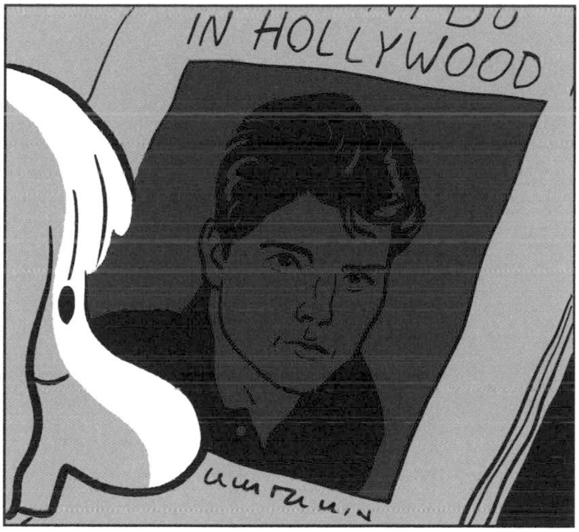
IN HOLLYWOOD

We were back in Brittany.

TOM CRUISE

THE MOST
HANDSOME ACTOR
IN HOLLYWOOD

Riad, are you coming?
I'm going to cut every-
body's hair!

PFFF

Can I get a different
haircut? I want to look like
Tom Cruise...

Ooh! That's
beyond my talents!

I'll take him to the
hairdresser in Pléhérel.
He'll know how to do it.

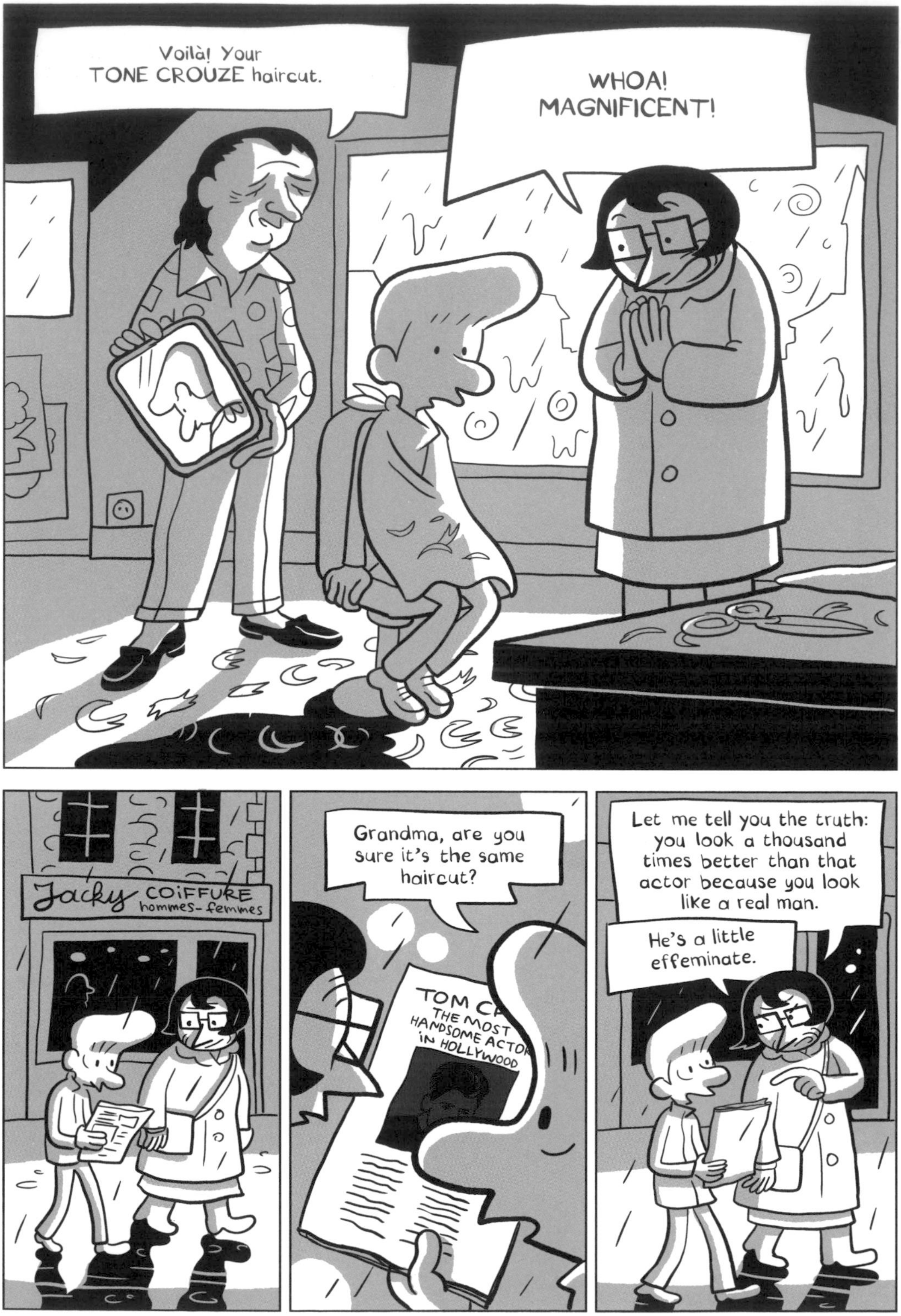
Voilà! Your TONE CROUZE haircut.
WHOA! MAGNIFICENT!
Jacky COIFFURE hommes-femmes
Grandma, are you sure it's the same haircut?
TOM CR
THE MOST HANDSOME ACTOR IN HOLLYWOOD
Let me tell you the truth: you look a thousand times better than that actor because you look like a real man.
He's a little effeminate.

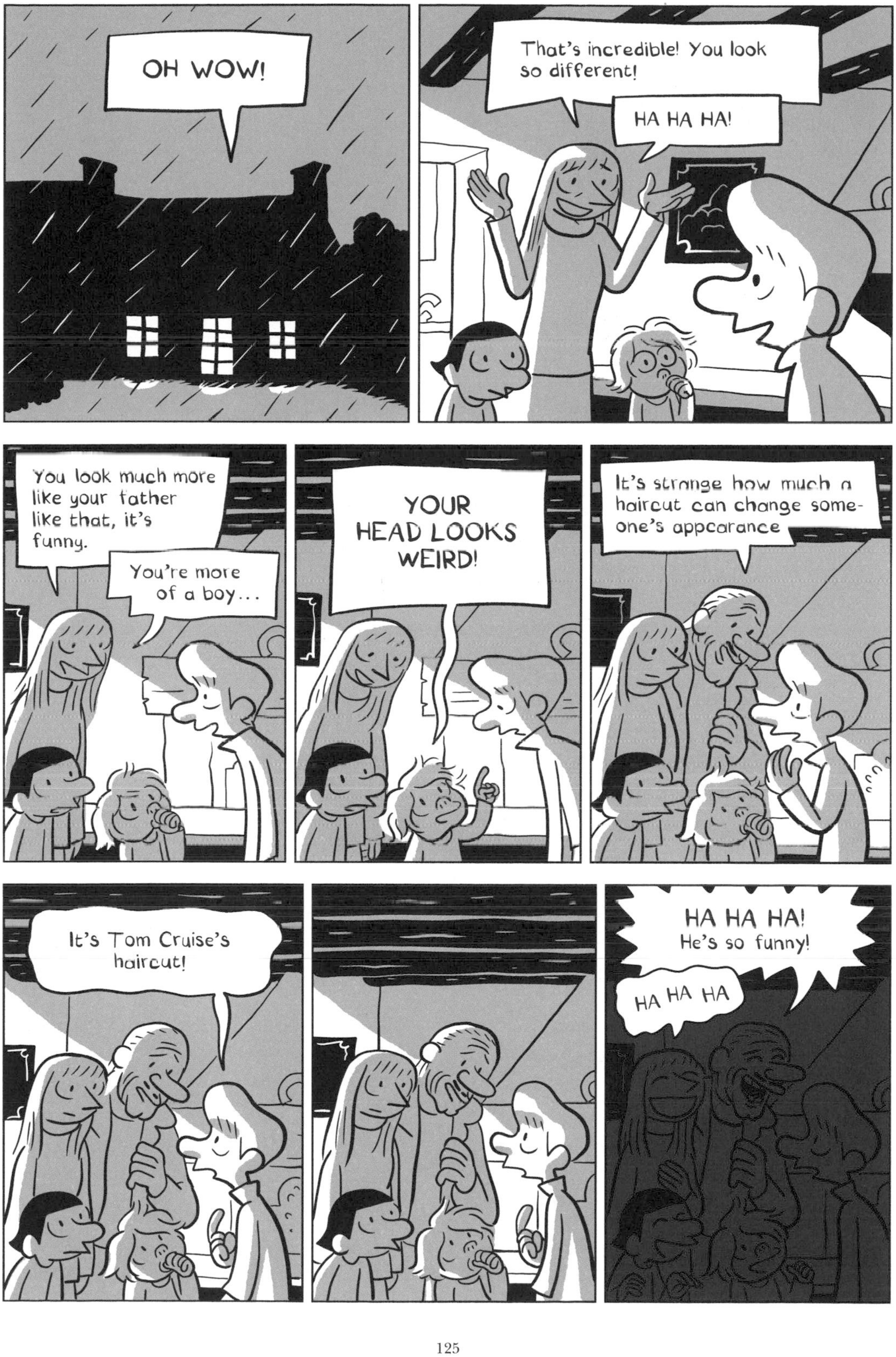
OH WOW!
That's incredible! You look so different!
HA HA HA!
You look much more like your father like that, it's funny.
You're more of a boy...
YOUR HEAD LOOKS WEIRD!
It's strange how much a haircut can change some-one's appearance
It's Tom Cruise's haircut!
HA HA HA! He's so funny!
HA HA HA

For years people had been complimenting me on my legendary beauty.

This time, nobody mentioned it.

Perhaps they had just forgotten?

Using the mirrors in my grandparents' bedroom, I was able to see myself in profile.

My skull looked like an egg!

Was it obvious?

Mama? I am handsome, aren't I?

Oh yes, very!

But stay humble, darling . . .

126

I was in fifth grade now, the last year in elementary school.

There was one other boy in fifth grade with me. His name was Nicolas. He was very nice.

Hi! I really like your hair!

I've got a new MSX game that my mother bought me on Saturday!

I played it all day long on Sunday, it's so cool

What's MSX?

It's a Japanese computer. You can come to my house and play it with me if you like!

A "COMPUTER"?

It's a machine that plugs into the TV and you can play on it with a joystick and...

OH YEAH?!? PLAYING ON THE TV?

COOOL!

But WHY did you cut your hair?

?!

It's Tom Cruise's haircut...

It's such a shame! Your hair was really nice before!

Nobody seemed to think my hair looked like Tom Cruise's. They probably didn't know who he was.

HA HA! I feel as if I have a new student in the class!

Sabrina, the prettiest girl in the school, no longer looked at me the same way

She influenced the others.

But who cared what the girls thought... My heart was already taken.

I was madly in love with Juliette, the main character in the cartoon show *Juliette Je t'aime*

Adapted from the manga by Rumiko Takahashi

It was a Japanese anime series that was on French TV every day.

"Juliette je t'aime! Juliette je t'aime! You really are the prettiest! Juliette je t'aime! And I know that you're my friend!" ♪ ♫ ♪ ♪ ♫

Juliette, a young widow, ran a guesthouse for students and young workers.

Among her boarders was Hugo, a shy, clumsy young boy.

Hugo was madly in love with Juliette but was incapable of telling her.

It went on for dozens of episodes and nothing happened. It was so romantic.

Hu... Hugo?

I identified completely with Hugo.

Like him, I was incapable of declaring my feelings to Juliette.

It was an impossible love.

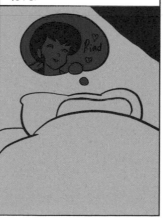

I was in love with a girl who didn't exist.

How could I spend my life with her?

129

Every other night, I dreamed that I was in Juliette's guesthouse.

Outside, the sky was full of stars.

Somebody was coming upstairs.

It was the REAL Juliette.

She wasn't just a drawing!

She came very close to my face.

I could see the little veins in her eyeballs.

I sat in her lap and touched the little chick on her apron.

Suddenly I realized that we were merging together.

I was part of her body.

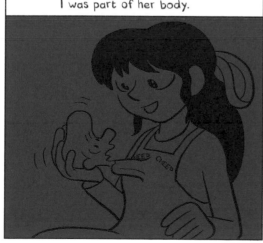

My mother and grandmother worked as a team. When one of them was depressed and negative...

You'll miss me when I'm dead...

...the other was cheerful and lighthearted.

Don't worry, you'll still be with us. I'm going to have you stuffed!

HA HA!

Sometimes one would be on the verge of tears...

I've done nothing with my life. I wasted my youth in Syria...

Petit Suisse!

...and then the other would make a joke, and they'd be laughing.

HA HA! Don't complain. I wasted mine in France...

HA HA HA

It was still depressing

My grandmother loved to go for walks in Saint-Servan, near Saint-Malo, where she'd lived when she was a child.

The Saint-Servan market! I used to go there before the war and there were so many stalls!

I used to just look. We'll go there one day!

Those were the good old days! I lived with my mama in a little apartment on Place de la Roulais...

And look at you, peeing on every corner, you naughty little monster!

All your family was from here. My grandfather came from Newfoundland! He would go out to sea in the bitter cold for months on end to fish cod...

We also have a Corsican in our background. Vincent Tranchant was his name. He was a lieutenant under Robert Surcouf.

Nothing bad can happen to us here. This city protects us, our ancestors are everywhere!

My grandmother had been less depressed since getting the dog. She talked to it as if it were human.

Lie on your back to get your belly tickled! Oh yes!

Ah, that rascal. He'd stay like that forever if he could, he loves it so much!

Happiest animal in the world

I liked going for walks in Saint-Servan. It was a mysterious place.

It was from Saint-Malo that my parents would take the ferry to Jersey.

AH! YOU'VE GOT A TIC!

?

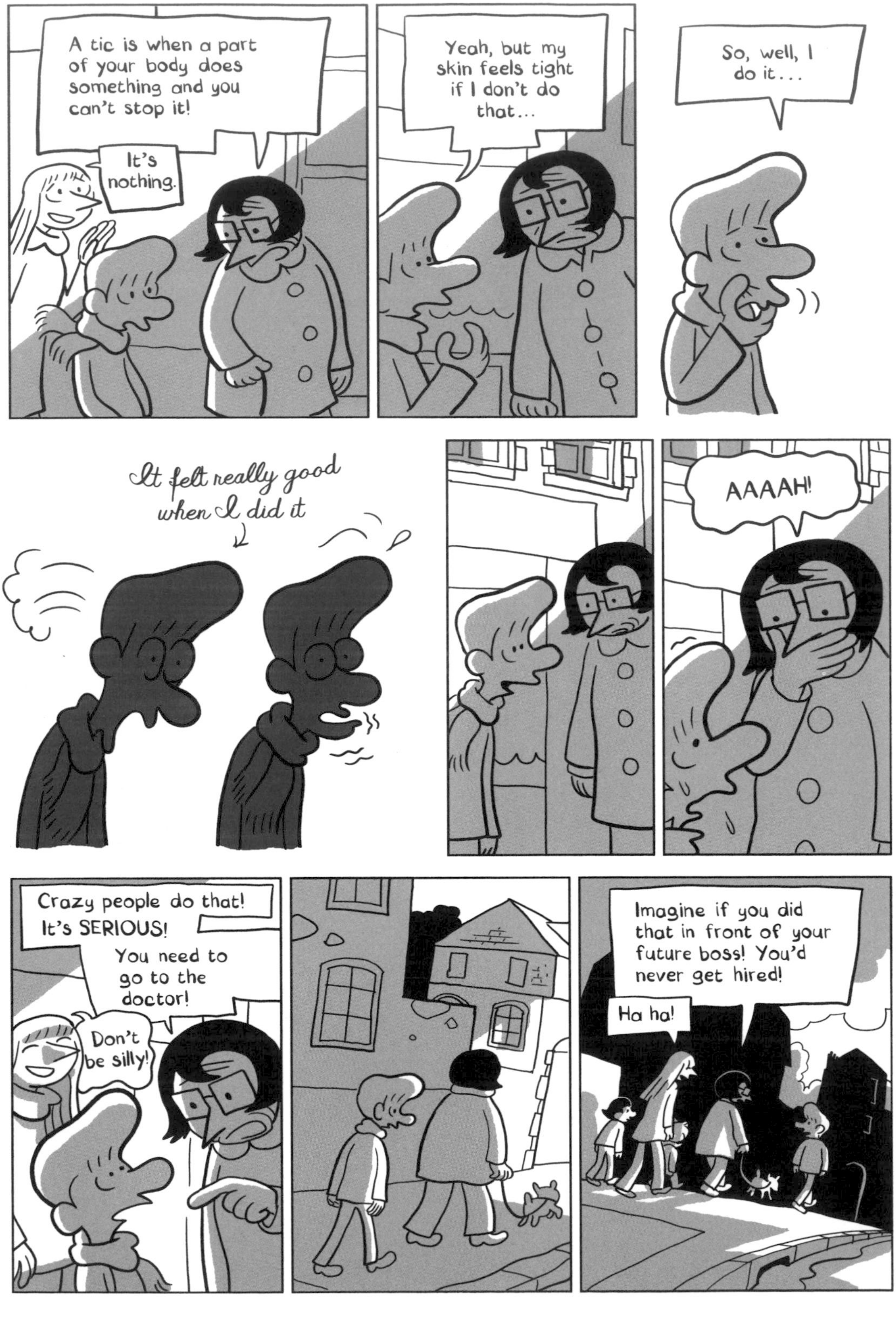
A tic is when a part of your body does something and you can't stop it!
It's nothing.
Yeah, but my skin feels tight if I don't do that...
So, well, I do it...
It felt really good when I did it
AAAAH!
Crazy people do that! It's SERIOUS!
You need to go to the doctor!
Don't be silly!
Imagine if you did that in front of your future boss! You'd never get hired!
Ha ha!

CHAPTER 5

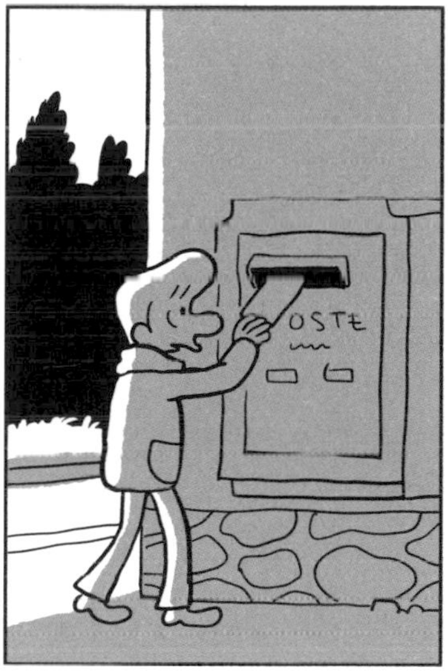
OSTE

In October 1988, my mother needed an emergency operation.

Her extreme tiredness wasn't just from her children.

She was seriously ill.

They operated yesterday. We should be able to see her tomorrow or the day after.

Cheer up everybody! I've made suckling pig to make us all feel better!

YUM!

The operation had gone well...

I could smell that horrible hospital smell even in the parking lot

...But the doctors were cautious: she had to undergo some long, difficult treatment, and the results were uncertain.

You see? They're the same bouquets we saw on that TV show!

OHHH!

THEY'RE SO PRETTY!

She looked strangely normal, maybe even better than before

I LOVE THESE FLOWERS!

My grandparents were very worried. They went to great efforts to hide this from us.

She'll be out of the hospital soon!

Watch out! The driver's about to overtake the guy in the lead!
Boys, watch me pull ahead!

My brothers looked worried, too. Everybody smiled in silence.

OH, HE'S SO FAST, YOUR GRANDPA!

Take it easy.

We'd been sleeping at my grandparents' house since my mother went to the hospital.

What would happen if she died?

Charles and my grandmother couldn't keep us . . .

. . . My father would come get us.

Would we go back to live in Ter Maaleh forever?

God is great!

Would I end up like Ahmad, the son of the Russian woman?

Would we all forget our lives from before?

There was a small statue of the Virgin Mary in our bedroom.

She looked like the women in Ter Maaleh ↓

I decided to pray to God to ask him to spare my mother.

Yes? Who is that?

He still looked like Georges Brassens →

I had the feeling he was going to ignore me. I'd ignored faith for so long.

What? Hello? I don't hear anything...

It seemed a bit too easy to ask him for help now that I had a problem.

Dear Santa, for my present this year I would like you to make my mama better. Thanks.

OSTE

Yes. I still believed. deep down ↘

And a cure!

I decided to behave perfectly forever ↗

Charles and my grandmother did all they could to take our minds off it.

They spoiled us rotten

But I could tell they were getting more and more worried.

When is Mama coming home?

I don't know, sweetie! Soon...

My mother had asked them not to tell my father.

RING!

She feared his reaction. She thought it would be better if she told him herself.

He'll call back next week!

Your mother will be home by then.

I didn't think it was a good idea not to tell him.

But nobody asked for my opinion.

Charles was fascinated by art.

Nothing better than being an artist and living from your talent.

Art is freedom! Look at that photograph! That's me when I was a guard.

THAT'S YOU?

After the war, I went to Morocco and opened a small photography shop in Mogador...

PHOTO

I took passport photos for a living, and on weekends I went out on my own and took pictures of nature ...

Oh, I wasn't a great photographer! But I wanted to forget the war and change my life...

One day I was in my shop and a very kind, impressive American man came in and asked if I would rent him my darkroom.

He explained that he'd just arrived in the area to shoot a movie, and that he'd have lots of film to develop...

Look, this is him. I'm on the left.

His name was Orson Welles.

He was shooting a movie called *Othello*.

Was he famous?

Oh yes, he was a great director! I agreed, of course. He didn't have enough money to make his movie, so I developed the film for free.

He would come to my darkroom, and we would have a drink together and chat.

He was incredible. He was directing and producing the movie, and playing the role of Othello... But it was complicated. He had no money. He would shoot for a while and then go back to act in Europe to fund his movie...

And the crew just waited for him...

They sunbathed all day

You see that pretty girl next to me in the photo? That's Suzanne Cloutier, the movie's lead actress. She was Peter Ustinov's wife. She liked me a lot, but I was too shy...

I was an extra in lots of scenes. For free, of course. Orson would change my outfit and shoot me from behind...

I said: "Orson, people will still be able to tell it's me, won't they?"

He laughed and said: "Charlie, stop asking questions and do what I tell you."

He explained to his set designer what he wanted, but the guy didn't understand, so Welles took the planks and nails and made it himself.

He could do anything! The man was a genius.

He was a visionary, a great artist who never gave up. A very gifted person.

Like you!

You have a GIFT, just like he did. You're very lucky.

I never saw Othello, though... It was never shown on TV. Speaking of which, it's time for my favorite game show!

After two weeks my mother came out of the hospital.

Impossible to tell that she was sick

Ooh, that hurts!

Come here, Fadi!

She was very tired but started looking for work again.

VRRRR

She had to start chemotherapy treatment.

I knew nothing about it. All I knew was that cancer was the most serious disease of all, and it was often fatal.

Juliette, what a lovely name!

Whenever I thought about it, an invisible hand squeezed my throat.

She's so cute, look at her...

RING

My mother called my father back...

Hello? Yes, I'm fine... And you? Yes, we missed a few of your calls, but it's okay. Everything's fine here.

I SAID: EVERYTHING'S FINE HERE.

...But she didn't tell him about the operation, or about her cancer.

My grandfather came to see us much more often once he found out his daughter was sick. All he talked about were horrible stories from the Second World War.

One day in June '44, I was in the center of Rennes with my friend Pierre, and there was a bombardment.

It was the Allies! They were aiming at the Krauts, but the bombs fell on us...I hid under a plow in the street, Pierrot went under a porch, there were explosions all around us...

We'd spent the day buying groceries in a supermarket in Langueux. It was just before Christmas. I noticed that there were more toys than usual in the aisles.

...and I heard SHRIEK!

I looked ahead: three feet from my spot, a huge shell had landed in the mud. It hadn't exploded. The mud had cushioned its fall.

Why were people buying toys at Christmas...?

But poor little Pierre died when the house he was in collapsed...

He died. I survived.

...when Santa would soon bring them to their homes for free?

Death! Death! We never know when it will strike! That's life!

Ooh, let's get salmon

ACH! SO SANTA DOESN'T REALLY EXIST? IT'S THE PARENTS WHO BUY ALL THE PRESENTS?

Well, yeah, bravo, but lower your voice so your brothers don't hear...

How come I didn't realize this before? I was supposed to be so clever!

You didn't really still believe in it, did you?

No, no!

Ooh, that's a hell of a tic!

God is the Santa of adults. He doesn't exist, but it makes people feel better to believe that he does...

You're a big boy now. You're learning all the adult secrets...

But if Santa didn't exist, who was going to save my mother?

Finally, my mother told my father.

WHAT? YOU'RE SICK?

As expected, he didn't take the news well.

SICK WITH WHAT? HOW DID YOU GET IT?

He yelled so loud we could all hear what he was saying.

IT'S THE FOOD, YOU MUST HAVE EATEN SOMETHING BAD!!!

STOP YELLING!

WHY DIDN'T YOU TELL ME RIGHT AWAY?!!

It wouldn't have changed anything! I didn't want to worry you.

You couldn't have done anything over there. It was better this way.

...dirty!

No, of course I'm not going to infect the children. It doesn't work like—

...unbelievable!

I AM VERY ANGRY!

OOOOH, VERY VERY VERY ANGRY!

CHAPTER 6

In February the school organized a ski trip in Auvergne, in the center of France.

It was the first time I'd left my mother.

Somehow I managed to hold back the tears

The other children looked happy to go ←

Nicolas went on about computers. I liked listening to him.

...on the MSX there's music while you're playing, but not on the Atari XE...

The elementary school from another village was on the trip, too.

The students looked older than us

Yet they were the same age

After an endless train ride, we arrived in La Bourboule.

Two group leaders welcomed us

Dominique

Gerard

Every day, we had to walk for a long time carrying our skis...

...before we could finally put them on and ski back to where we'd started.

There wasn't enough snow

Cross-country skiing was the most exhausting thing I'd ever done.

At night we slept in an all-boys dormitory.

Can't feel my legs

I got to know Yannick and his friends.

Tomorrow I'm going to tell her I love her.

For sure.

No, I will!

Okay, we'll both tell her we love her. She can choose!

Yeah, okay.

?

But I love her, too!

Hey, who are you talking about?

Tiphaine, the prettiest girl in our school!

We're all in love with her!

She's the most incredible, brilliant girl in the world!

A beauty!

Oh Tiphaiiiine, I'd do this to her, like this.

Ohh

As soon as you see her you'll fall in love!

But she's ours, so hands off!

We were there first!

Oh Tiphaine, my love...

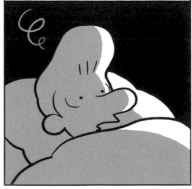
They felt what I felt for Juliette, but for a real girl in their class!

The next day...

That's her!

Oh Tiphaine... Tiphaine, my love...

Look at her ponytail swinging...

She's got a strange face, Tiphaine. Her friend is prettier, don't you think?

What'd he say?

What did you say?

HUH?

SHUT YOUR MOUTH! Don't insult Tiphaine, asshole!

Fag!

No, I was just kidding...

PRICK!

They took it so seriously that I decided not to say anything else.

I'm going to tell her I love her right now!

Tiphaine was skinny. She was gap-toothed and had an endless forehead.

Hi, Tiphaine! Can I tell you something?

She never smiled and she always looked angry. How could anyone be in love with her?

I love you!

Yeah, that's great, thanks, but DON'T TALK TO ME.

A few days later, Nicolas started showing an interest in Tiphaine.

It's true, she's pretty. I think I love her!

I didn't want to feel left out, so I joined in.

HEY! THAT'S IT. I'M IN LOVE WITH TIPHAINE, TOO!

AH NO, NOT ANOTHER ONE! You see, I told you!

She bewitches all the guys...

Are you going to tell her?

Um no, I'm too shy.

Good.

You wouldn't stand a chance anyway.

She could have anybody she wants.

I realized that Yannick had the Tom Cruise haircut that I had wanted.

I'm going to tell her I love her again soon

A party had been organized for the last night.

The MSX is currently the most popular model in Japan, even if NEC is trying to . . .

Unbelievable: girls and boys were allowed to dance together!

The chaperones were the only ones dancing

The students were drinking Oasis

After a while the girls started dancing too. The boys just leaned against the wall.

Of course, the Amiga 500 has the HAM mode, but it's so expensive that.

"I'm looking for a little warmth to put in my heaaart"

Suddenly Tiphaine appeared.

"They carry me to the end of the night"

Gérard, the group leader, asked her to dance.

"The demons of midniiiight"

Her expression never changed ↓

Where did they learn to dance like that?

"Carry me to insomnia"

Suddenly Yannick started dancing with Dominique.

"The phantoms of boredom"

Everybody watched the two couples.

"Carry me to the end of the night"

What would my Syrian cousins think if they could see this now?

"The demons of midnight"

I looked at the other girls.

They were all fixated on Yannick and didn't look at me.

Perhaps one of them secretly loved me?

The song ended →

Tiphaine walked past Yannick. He grabbed her arm.

Tiphaine.

I really need to know if you love me or not. That's all.

Yes. I love you.

I could not understand how a boy my age could say that to a girl.

Tiphaine didn't smile all night, and the two lovers didn't speak to each other again.

Her expression never changed →

She loves me, damn it, she loves me

I realized I was incapable of saying "I love you" to anybody.

Even thinking about it made me blush

Where you going?

Since I pretended to love Tiphaine, I couldn't stop thinking about her.

I'm going to see Tiphaine in the girls' dorm

Watch out.

Riad is the one I really love

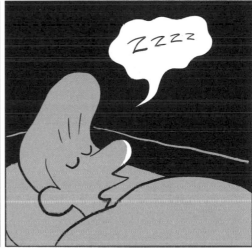

ZZZZ

HEY, GUYS, LISTEN! YOU WON'T BELIEVE IT! I went to the girls' dorm and I saw Tiphaine!

AND? AND?

She saw me, she said shhh, she lifted up her T-shirt, and I SAW HER BREASTS!

WHOOOA!

WOW!!!! HOT!!!

I couldn't wait to go home.

I scanned the crowd for my mother and my grandparents.

When suddenly, at the end of the platform, standing apart from the other parents ...

I hadn't even known that my father was supposed to come back from Saudi Arabia.

Your mother is a little tired. She's resting.

She's looking after your brothers

I came in OUR car!

Beautiful, huh?

It's really small!!!

?

What do you mean "It's really small"?

It's a Golf! It's very expensive. It's a high-quality German car!

You're so spoiled! At your age I didn't even have shoes!

And I wasn't going to spend 70,000 francs on a sedan when I don't even live here!

We drove in silence for a while.

I hope you were careful with WOMEN on your trip?

Um yeah

European women can give you AIDS if you're not careful. AIDS is a terrible disease that kills people with no morals!

You can catch it LIKE THAT!

CLICK CLACK

So that's why you should avoid women.

Do you think about women sometimes?

No

Sniffff

Well, that's a good thing, thanks be to God.

We DESIRE women, and that is man's great weakness! We'd be much better off if they didn't exist.

Even just seeing them—ooooh, it can set you off.

And here in France, the women are too easy...

They have no modesty, no morals...

I had LOTS of women, LOTS, before your mother! I was manipulated by them...

French women without honor...you can pick them up like that!

They gave themselves to every man, one after another, like that!

CLICK
CLACK

A Syrian woman would NEVER do that. NEVER. Not even a Christian.

I've got a safe-deposit box in a bank in Paris, and inside there's a plastic bag with photos of all the women I've had!

Sniff

Ha ha ha ha
PFFFFFT...

My father seemed nervous.

He accelerated for no reason . . .

VRRR

He muttered things in Arabic, jerked the steering wheel sideways...

LAAA Ana ma badé ya...

...and braked suddenly

I felt sick, so I opened the window, and a foul stench filled the car.

YOU SMELL THAT? IT'S PIG SHIT!

The French spread it over their fields as fertilizer!

Smells good, huh?

What smells better, here or Ter Maaleh? Be honest!

FRANCE! The land of infidels and pigs!

Even the vegetables that grow here are full of pork!

My father's visit went smoothly. He was on vacation. The atmosphere grew calmer.

We were living in the remote holiday home again →

Oooh look at Sheikh Bab El Ehr—he looks like my brother Hadj Mohamed

My mother kept applying for jobs. My father didn't say anything.

Oooh, nice handwriting!

He bought groceries at the village

...came to fetch us from school...

Look! A thrush! They're delicious...Oh no, it's just a starling.

Sometimes he even did laundry.

Of course, he never mentioned my mother's illness.

I thought he was overdoing it.

Nooo, leave it. I'll wash up.

Thanks, that's nice.

I had the feeling he blamed my mother for getting sick.

I can do this, I'm a very modern man.

She needed medical care and we were stuck in France.

You have to get better quickly...

My father gave my mother a little more money.

Look, here's 300 francs for the end of the month...

Why don't you make a monthly bank transfer? It'd be simpler...

Really?

BOUKRA.

HAHA

HA HA

Boukra means "tomorrow" in Arabic. It's a word that's used to indicate laziness, a tendency to put everything off to tomorrow and end up doing nothing.

Transfers cost money. I'd rather give you cash when you need it...

My mother drove herself to the hospital for her treatment.

We stayed at home with my father.

Riad. Have you ever seen your mother's doctors?

No!

What do you mean "no"? You've never gone with her to the hospital?

Well, no.

THEN HOW DO WE KNOW THAT SHE REALLY GOES THERE?

Where else would she go?

Women need to be watched.

Do you read the Quran sometimes? Want to read it now?

Um, no, not really.

WHAT?

You're not a little boy anymore, you know! It's time you took an interest in religion! In Saudi Arabia I learned things, I understood things...

I listened to the wisest Muslims on cassette tapes, and it opened my eyes...

Don't you want to try praying?

AT LEAST TRY!

Um, well, pfff... I don't know.

We're Muslims. We should pray.

But I'm a liberal, so I won't force you. One day I'm sure it will come to you.

God has not decided that this is the moment. He and only he decides where and when things happen.

He just hasn't decided yet that this is the right moment for you.

I'm glad you cut your hair. That's a real man's haircut.

At 8 pm my father sat in front of the TV to watch the news.

The prime minister, Michel Rocard, left the council meeting without talking to reporters

He looked worried, and he took notes in Arabic about what he watched.

Look at all those socialists and Commies! I'd have them all up against the wall... The only great French politician alive today is LE PEN! He loves his country. He's a nationalist! But he'll never get elected, poor guy. The French love Negroes too much!

Compared to them, they feel intelligent.

OH! Riad! Look! That's Saddam Hussein! The greatest Arab politician alive today! A Sunni, like us! The president of Iraq, the most modern Arab country in the world.

With more than a million dead, the Iran-Iraq War is undoubtedly one of the worst conflicts of the second half of the ...

Every year for the past 15 years, I've applied for a teaching job at the University of Baghdad.

But I never got a reply...

Ah, thanks be to God, I will keep trying.

You never told me that.

I don't tell you everything! I am a man of many mysteries ...

So, did Saddam Hussein win the war against the Iranians, Papa?

OF COURSE he won! He showed what we are capable of.

There's nothing worse than the Iranians, the Shiites and their mullahs... They think they're better than the rest of the world, but they'll see! We should dig a hole for Khomeini and his gang, put a bullet in the backs of their necks, then bury them in the hole. They're our enemies, like the Israelis.

Saddam Hussein is a man of the people, and now he's the president. He has a vision for the Arabs. He is a great NATIONALIST!

He grew up in a crappy little village. He had no father, poor kid, and his stepfather beat him all the time. And so did the other children in the village...

But at 12 he ran away to live with his uncle, who was a teacher and who taught him everything. SCHOOL! SCHOOL! It's the most important thing of all!

After that, he carried off a brilliant coup d'état and became the great president he is now... Legend has it that once he was in power, he sought out those children who used to beat him and had them all executed.

HEE HEE HEE HEE!

He modernized his country, built roads, schools... He even won a prize from UNESCO for his battle against ignorance ...UNESCO! Even the Americans supported him. But then they abandoned him to support Israel, the dogs!

Saddam and I, we've had the same life. For me, it was Hadj Mohamed who beat me when I was a boy. One day he threw a watermelon at my ribs for no reason! Ooooh, that hurt!

Seriously, if I touch the spot where that watermelon hit me, it still hurts now.

But if I ever pulled off a coup d'état and become president, I wouldn't have him executed. After all, he's my brother...

My grandmother invited us over for lunch. She hadn't seen my father for more than a year.

Abdel! How nice to see you!

Yes, yes, nice to see you too...

Moustik was excited by all these visitors.

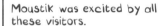

Nobody on earth had ever been so pleased to see us

Rff Rff Rff

His joy was infectious.

Rff Rff Rff

Agggh

Rff Rff

AAAWW

BAM

WHAT IS WRONG WITH YOU?!

Sorry. I thought he was attacking me! I'm scared of dogs!

THAT'S NO REASON TO KICK HIM!

I didn't kick him umm...

My father's kick cast a pall over the meal.

My father ate all his vegetables...

...but pushed the roast pork to the side of his plate with his napkin

I ate as if nothing had happened.

I avoided his disapproving look (I loved roast pork)

My father acted aloof, which he never had before.

He drank his water very seriously

When he talked to me about religion he had the same worried expression as some of the children in Ter Maaleh.

Exaggerated expression of all-knowing wisdom

As if, surrounded by our sins...

...his forbearance and morality...

...would silently teach us a lesson.

When the church bells rang, my father made strange noises to drown out the sound.

DING DONG! DING DONG!

SHLURP

TSKK SHLUP

He looked around as if he were being watched...

...and checked the time every five minutes

Before dessert, he left the table.

What's he doing?

He's gone to pray...

Tap   Tap

DING DONG DING DONG

CHAPTER 7

Before I started middle school, my mother decided to move the family to Rennes, a city 60 miles from Cap Fréhel.

She hoped she'd be able to find work there. My father had gone back to Saudi Arabia.

Rennes was a gray place, but you could smell the sea in the distance

She rented an apartment in the southern part of the city, on Rue Paul Bourget.

My grandfather cosigned the lease and bought almost all the furniture.

And most important: THE TV.

My brothers shared a large bedroom...

"I walked along the avenue, heart open to the sky so blue ..."

Fadi loved to sing

...and I had my own.

With flower-patterned wallpaper

173

Fadi's kindergarten was right across from the apartment building.

I'll see you from my window!

Yahya's elementary school was 100 yards down the road.

It looks nice, with those little windows

As for me, I would not go to the nearest middle school.

When I got there to enroll you, there was a big group of children outside, Arabs, foreigners, sitting on a bench, and one of them spat at my feet and laughed...

Believe me, the kids I saw outside that school were EXACTLY THE SAME as the ones at your school in Syria.

I felt as if I were still in Ter Maaleh and I thought: "No way am I sending my son here."

You WON'T GO!

I didn't really see what my mother was talking about.

I only ever left the apartment to go to the local park with Yahya

All the people I had ever seen in that park were white.

Finally, my mother enrolled me in another middle school, located ten bus stops from our house.

The assistant principal gave us the tour. We felt important.

Here we have the library, the cafeteria, the study hall, the student common room...

I was a little afraid of going to that school...

It'll make a nice change from Ter Maaleh and Cap Fréhel...

There were sequoia trees in the yard

Wasn't it going to be too difficult?

My grandfather was very anxious about my starting school.

You'll meet some real jerks in middle school, but it'll be okay.

There are always some guys who don't like you and want to beat you up...

Big boys...

But that's life, and you have to deal with it. There are nice people and there are assholes. Mostly assholes, in fact. But that's humanity for you.

My advice: don't get in fights, because you're bound to lose. You're not tough enough...

Keep your head down...

...but most important...

YOU HAVE TO START GOING OUT WITH GIRLS NOW!

Look out for the prettiest ones, the ones with the nicest curves...

...go over and seduce them by paying them compliments...

...and KISS THEM! That's what we're like in this family!

Yuck

Aarrgh you're not gay, are you?

No!

Well, then!

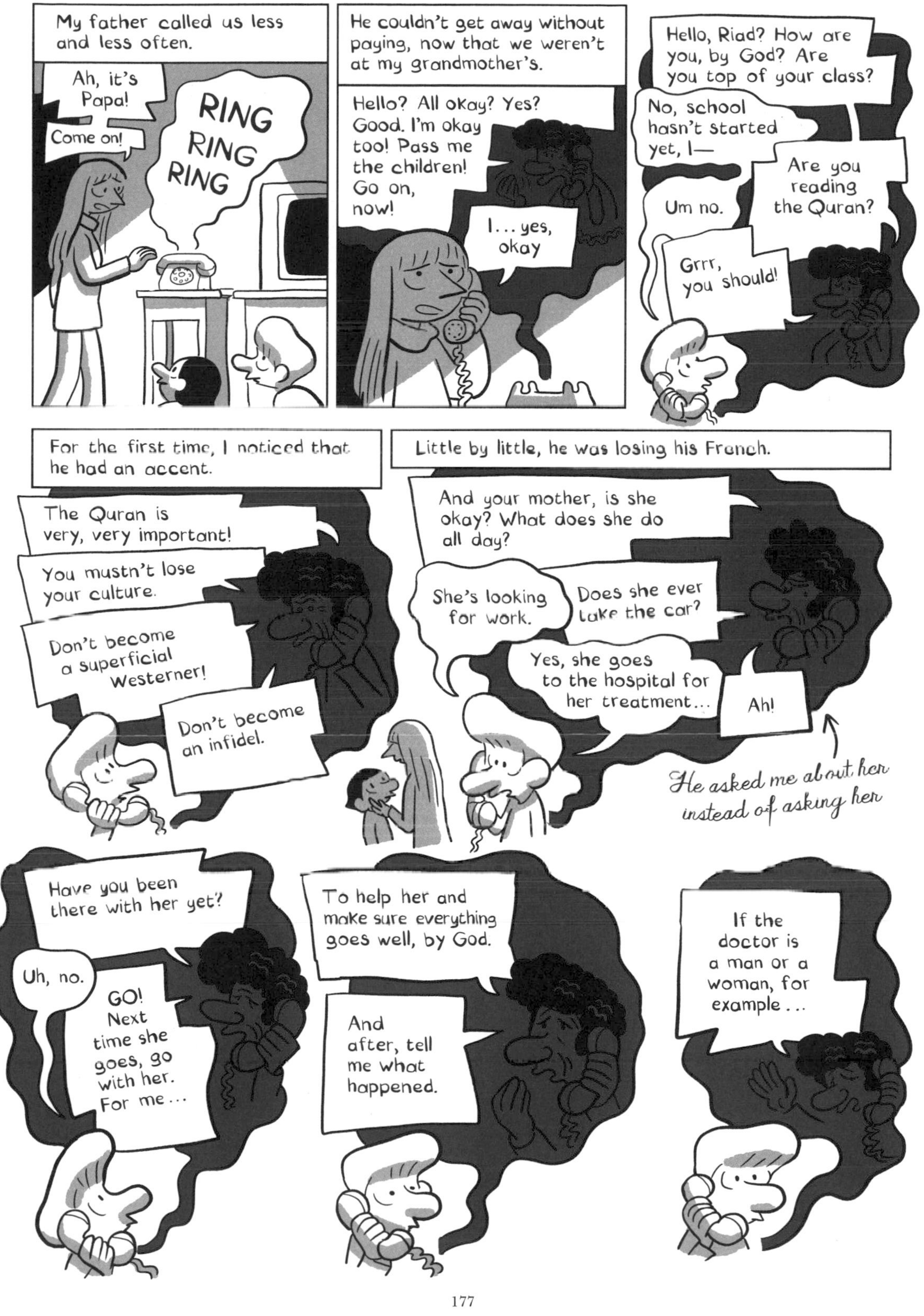

My father called us less and less often.
Ah, it's Papa!
Come on!
RING RING RING
He couldn't get away without paying, now that we weren't at my grandmother's.
Hello? All okay? Yes? Good. I'm okay too! Pass me the children! Go on, now!
I... yes, okay
Hello, Riad? How are you, by God? Are you top of your class?
No, school hasn't started yet, I—
Are you reading the Quran?
Um no.
Grrr, you should!
For the first time, I noticed that he had an accent.
The Quran is very, very important!
You mustn't lose your culture.
Don't become a superficial Westerner!
Don't become an infidel.
Little by little, he was losing his French.
And your mother, is she okay? What does she do all day?
She's looking for work.
Does she ever take the car?
Yes, she goes to the hospital for her treatment...
Ah!
He asked me about her instead of asking her
Have you been there with her yet?
Uh, no.
GO! Next time she goes, go with her. For me...
To help her and make sure everything goes well, by God.
And after, tell me what happened.
If the doctor is a man or a woman, for example...

On the first day of school, there was a huge crowd of people and several sixth-grade classes.

6A   6B   6C   *Nobody singing the national anthem*   6D

The other students were all white. I didn't see anybody of a different race.

Some of them seemed to know each other already   *They looked healthy*

Our teacher came to fetch us and led us down a corridor.

She looked like a madwoman, and her hair was dyed with henna

Come on children, this way! This way!

In the classroom, she took attendance.

Kalouec?
Here
Laennec?
Yes
Boudet?
Yes

Hortey?
Here
Sattouf?
Yesss!

HAHA HA HA HA

Ohmigod   Sa-what?

I decided to act as if nobody had laughed.

All right, calm down! Take out some paper and write down the names and professions of your parents.

Heh

Pssst!

Riad Sattouf
Mother: housewife
Father: great profes...

Is your name really The Pubes?

Sattouf, not la touffe

Ha, so you're called Her Pubes, ha!

His name was Titouan.

She explained to us that we would take lots of different classes, each one with a different teacher.

You'll have to get organized! You're not babies anymore—fifth grade is over.

It was all new and exciting.

Eager to be the best

At recess, we went out to the yard.

I headed toward a small group of my classmates who were talking together.

Titouan was at the center and did most of the talking.

When I was in fifth grade, I snogged every chick in the school!

Hey, what does "snog" mean?

HA HA HA!

Mr. Pubes don't know what it means...

It means kissing a girl with your tongue...

SERIOUSLY?

Shit, are you a little kid or what?

Hey, we're too young to talk about that!

No, we're not! I'll teach you whenever you're ready!

EEEEEEEK

It was class after class for the rest of the day.

Roadec?

Yes.

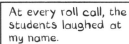

At every roll call, the students laughed at my name.

Sattouf?

HA HA

HA HA HA

His pubes, ha ha!

And yet Titouan had a ridiculous name too...

JUVERT?

Yeah, I'm here.

Nobody laughed or called him Green Juice

Nobody cared about my origins, but they were intrigued by my first name.

Where does "Riad" come from?

It's Syrian, um... it comes from Syria

Huh? What?

Is that a real country? I've never heard of it!

It's a funny name anyway.

After lunch, I started drawing on a bench in the middle of the yard.

That attracted the girls

Oh my God, that's REALLY REALLY good. Seriously, are you a pro or what?

WHOA!

Will you draw something for me?

Oh, look at that. Mr. Pubes likes to draw HA HA!

Stop showing off...

It's not that great anyway. I've got a cousin who draws better, ha ha.

Even so, I soon had the reputation of being the school's artist.

The weeks passed. I was good friends with the girls in my class. Céline and Vanessa never left me alone.

In the morning they would kiss me on the cheek!

I could smell their scent of soap and sweat on my cheek all day.

I thought about them all the time.

I began to realize that I was haunted.

Kiss

Kiss

I became obsessed with a model I saw in a TV commercial.

Her name was Cindy Crawford.

Where did it come from, this attraction?

Was I normal.

Her face reminded me of my cousin Qamar in Syria.

Yes, Qamar was more beautiful than Cindy Crawford

I started cutting her photos out of magazines and sticking them on my wall.

My new passion made somebody happy.

Look at what I bought you! Who's a lucky boy, eh?

My mother was tired out by her treatment.

She took care of us all day long and received nothing but rejection letters from potential employers.

Thankfully I was brilliant

"An interested and interesting student!" Bravo, darling!

We lived on 2500 francs per month and we never wanted for anything.

We went shopping at a mall called the Alma Center

That was where I was given, without knowing what they were, a pair of Nike sneakers.

Go ahead! They're yours!

They were Day Glo yellow

184

A longhaired kid from another class came over to talk to me.

Cool shoes, man. Shame they're not AIR, but I love the color.

You're into skateboarding, right?

His name was Cédric.

I love skating. My dad's got a Gold Wing motorcycle, what about yours? No, huh... One day I'll have one too...

You wanna go skating after school?

So we started skateboarding in the streets when school was over.

He was my only male friend

He held forth endlessly. Whenever he asked me a question, he answered it for me.

I'm training myself to do back-flips, you ever done those? No, huh, it's really hard, you need good momentum.

School finished early, so we had plenty of time.

I love remote-controlled cars. Do you have any? No? I've got several.

I loved going fast

FUCK OFF, YOU FAG!

Son of a bitch!

They were younger than us, but there were more of them.

ARABS! LET'S GET OUT OF HERE!

Hey, this is a street for everybody. We're allowed to be here.

What did you say, fag?

WATCHASAY?

I'm gonna take your board, you sonofabitch.

FUCK YOUR MOTHER, YOU FAG!!!

ARE YOU CRAZY? WHY'D YOU TALK BACK?!

When we were out of sight, we caught our breath.

They're Arabs. You need to steer clear of them.

But we didn't do anything.

That's their territory. We shouldn't have gone that way!

But why did they attack us?

They're Arabs. That's how they all are, looking for trouble...

Hey! I'm an Arab and I'm not like that!

HA HA! You're not an Arab!

You're a French kid with an Arab name...

You're not a real Arab...

Why didn't you speak to them in Arabic if you're an Arab?

I can't speak it anymore, I've forgotten it.

See? You're not an Arab.

Arabs are always in gangs. They attack people and steal their money. You need to stay away from their territory. They kill people for nothing...

?!?

187

I continued to be a very good student. I did everything my teachers asked of me.

Riad, 19 out of 20. Perfect, except your handwriting is perhaps a little too small.

Our homeroom teacher was also our French teacher. She was a little bit hippy-ish and very outgoing. I loved to impress her.

Have you seen anything this weekend that surprised you, that moved you, that made you laugh? Something poetic?

Who wants to go first? Go ahead, don't be afraid!

Yes, Riad.

I saw a funny guy on a moped who was pulling a little trailer with a little rabbit inside it.

OHHHH!

That's VERY sweet, surprising, and unusual . . .

Yes, Titouan?

Me too, mith. I thaw a widdle wabbit behind a moped and I wuv telling you about it in my thilly widdle fag voice.

HA HA HA HA HA HA HA HA HA

I had never noticed that there was anything unusual about my voice. But Titouan's imitation was eerily accurate, and the whole class seemed to agree.

Oh yes, oh all riiiight...

HAHA HAHA

I realized by now that "fag" was the worst insult imaginable.

I don't want to hear words like that in my class, Titouan. It's unacceptable.

Sorry, miss, but he really does have a fag's voice! I couldn't help myself!

BUT WE DO NOT SAY "FAG'S VOICE"! It's not nice! Where are your manners? Do you even know what a fag is?

Well, yeah. Its thumb-one who talks like thith.

Just because Riad has an effeminate voice doesn't make him a subject of mockery!

Everybody has a right to be the way they are!

I would also advise you to be more like Riad, who participates in class.

He's an example to you.

Okay, mith. I'll talk thumb more aboud Mr. Pubes' widdle wabbit behind da moped.

HA HAHA HA HA HA HA HA

189

After lunch I went to the library to draw. It was a quiet place. The only noises were the shouts of the boys playing soccer in the yard.

Pass, dickhead paaasss!

Hey, Riad! I wanted to ask you something! Would you...

um, draw something just for me?

A nice drawing that I ...could um put on the wall above my bed.

Above her bed! I started work on it that evening.

I showed her the work in progress the next day.

WOW, IT'S FANTASTIC!

I'll finish it tonight and give it to you tomorrow.

VERY DANGEROUS SLOPE

When I'd finished, I showed it to my mother.

WHOOOA! It's the best drawing you've ever done!

Will you give it to me? I'm going to frame it and put it in my room!

Sure, okay!

The next day, Vanessa swooped in on me.

So, have you got my drawing?

Oh, I gave it to my mother! She really wanted it.

It's really nice of you to do that. She must be so happy!

I'll do another one for you!

Nah, don't bother

?

So, what's happening with you two?

He gave his drawing to his mother

HA HA nooo!

What a shmuck.

Ha, that's puthetic . . .

Come with me, will you? I need to pee.

Yeah.

Vanessa and Céline didn't speak to me after that.

From that day on, my life changed.

The boys, led by Titouan, ate here

The girls here

I tried to sit with Vanessa and Céline...

Uh, sorry. This seat is taken.

Go away, please, and thank you.

I sat at another table.

The girls next to me moved away.

I dropped my fork.

TiNG

When I pushed my chair back, it banged into the chair of the student behind me.

In retaliation, he shoved his chair back really hard.

CRACK

AAAGGHHH

BOOHOOOOHOO

The assistant principal took me to the nurse's office.

BOOHOOOOOO

Shame of the century

Ugh, no. What a mess he's making.

It's nothing. You'll have a false tooth, that's all.

I have lots of false teeth.

My father came back from Saudi Arabia for a few weeks.

"...ooh the Champs-Élysées"

There's no need to get so worked up about it!

Mama, who's that?

WORKED UP?! HE SPENDS FIVE YEARS AT SCHOOL IN TER MAALEH, "THE WORST SCHOOL IN THE WORLD," AND IT'S HERE IN FRANCE THAT SOME NASTY FRENCH SHIT KNOCKS MY SON'S TOOTH OUT!

OF COURSE I'M WORKED UP! YOU SHOULD HAVE TURNED AROUND AND STABBED THAT DOG IN THE EYE WITH YOUR KNIFE!

The insurance will pay for the false tooth.

WHAT FALSE TOOTH! My son is disfigured! What false tooth!

NASTY FRENCH SHIT!

My son has lost his tooth, he has tics like some mentally handicapped person, nude photos of women in his bedroom, and this apartment is tiny...

It's all we can afford with the money you give us!

Buy us a house if you have enough money!

Ooh la la, by God I'm so tired...

"Oooh Champs-Élysées!"

And that one singing Joe Dassin all day long...

I know I've been very tough with money, but it means you receive the Family Allowance benefit...

Heuk!

...and it makes me happy that France has to pay us, that we PROFIT from the state's money.

Because France has you, and I don't!

If you could just give me 1,000 francs extra, that would be perfect!

I'll talk to my bank about it, I'll talk to my bank...

I tried to imagine my parents living together as old, retired people. I felt certain it would never happen.

The five of us went for walks in the center of Rennes.

My father hardly ever smiled MUTU

He was filled with rage. He hated everything he saw.

Look at this place, dog shit everywhere! It's dirtier than Ter Maaleh!

HA HA, it's my plane, you moron, HA HA!

RIAD! Leave Yayha alone! He treats the poor kid like Hadj Mohamed used to treat me!

GIVE IT BACK!

Always tormenting me because I was smaller and weaker!

SOCIÉTÉ GÉNÉRALE

RIAD! YAHYA! STOP RUNNING!

OR THE NEGRO WILL EAT YOU!

DISQUES

I was sure the man heard what my father said.

He hurried across the road →

Stay close to us! Where are your manners!

We're not monkeys!

Will you stop yelling?!

Look at our cousins over there!

It's the Frenchies of the future hee hee!

Are they Syrian?

No, they're Algerian or Moroccan, I think...

When they speak Arabic it sounds awful, like they're retarded... They're only here for the welfare hee hee!

By God, if they were at least believers... but look at those kids! Dressed like American gangsters! I bet they're bottom of the class...

I've had enough of your racist outbursts in front of the kids!

Okayy, okayyy!

Riad! You know what I like about the Jews? There's one thing they do VERY WELL and that we Arabs should copy.

?

They're VERY DEMANDING with their children.

They look after them, care about their education, and always expect them to be top of the class.

That's why I'm very demanding with you. You HAVE to be as good as the Jews.

They know how the world works.

Yeah, and they give their wives enough money, too!

The French are something else. They think they're superior and don't want to work. So they bring in North Africans and Negroes to do the jobs they don't like. That was Mitterrand's idea and the socialist traitors...

But there's one thing the French didn't think about. The North Africans and the Negroes are really good at one thing: having kids! HA HA! See, that's what happens when you don't love your country. Other people come and take it from you!

I'm telling you, in 100 years, there'll be nobody here but North Africans and Negroes.

WELL DONE, FRANCE! HA HA HA HA HA!

August 1990: we were on vacation at my grandmother's house.

UNBELIEVABLE! INCREDIBLE NEWS!

SADDAM HUSSEIN HAS INVADED KUWAIT! TAKE THAT, AMERICA!!!

Saddam Hussein had launched a surprise attack on Kuwait, accusing them of stealing oil from Iraq. The two countries shared an oil field on the border.

He was fulfilling the dream of Iraq's nationalist Baath Party, which considered Kuwait to be an illegitimate state created by the British.

May God help him! Saddam is a genius.

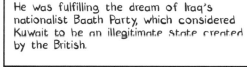

But still, attacking a country like that—it's horrible.

PFFT. YOU KNOW NOTHING ABOUT IT! It's a fake country invented by the Western bastards so that they could have more oil!

Historically, Kuwait belonged to Mesopotamia. It's a province of Iraq. Saddam is taking it back, quite rightly. It's not up to the West to make decisions for the Arabs.

We Arabs must take back our destiny, with the aid of God, from the imperialist Westerners who humiliate us and protect Israel.

Saddam is the pride of the Arabs! Ooooh this is great!

I had the impression that my father thought he'd played a role in what was happening in Kuwait. As if he'd advised Saddam, who was simply acting on his ideas.

The Americans won't react. Saddam has one of the most powerful armies in the world. And he'll win the psychological war.

HE GAVE THEM A SLAP!

Hee hee, how satisfying it must be to make a decision that changes history!

Iraq's invasion of Kuwait is a DAZZLING act of foreign policy.

CHAPTER 8

Five months later... contrary to my father's predictions, an international coalition attacked the Iraqi army.

It was Operation Desert Storm.

Mytics had been replaced by acne

When George Bush launched the attack, we felt as if it were the beginning of World War Three.

But the Iraqi army was swept away in record time.

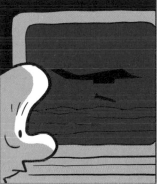

Saddam Hussein launched missiles at American military bases in Saudi Arabia, where my father was still teaching.

He was brought back on a French military jet. I thought he was fleeing the bombardments.

But he admitted that he'd been fired by the University of Riyadh.

He's Papa, right?

All that because I made a joke in the teachers' lounge about the emir of Kuwait.

Ha ha! And Emir Jaber! He sees the Iraqi army coming and he runs off to his Western masters with his tail between his legs. Ha ha ha!

None of those dogs laughed, and one of them repeated what I'd said to the university president.

You're lucky—we can't put you in prison because you have a French passport. NOW GET THE HELL OUT!

Saudi Arabia, a country of collaborators under the American thumb, no pride, traitors, cowards... It's all screwed up...

Saddam Hussein's defeat devastated my father.

Everything is screwed up. The Americans have won.

The West destroyed the Arab world! One day the West will pay for this, may God help us.

I give up. I'm going to look for a job in France.

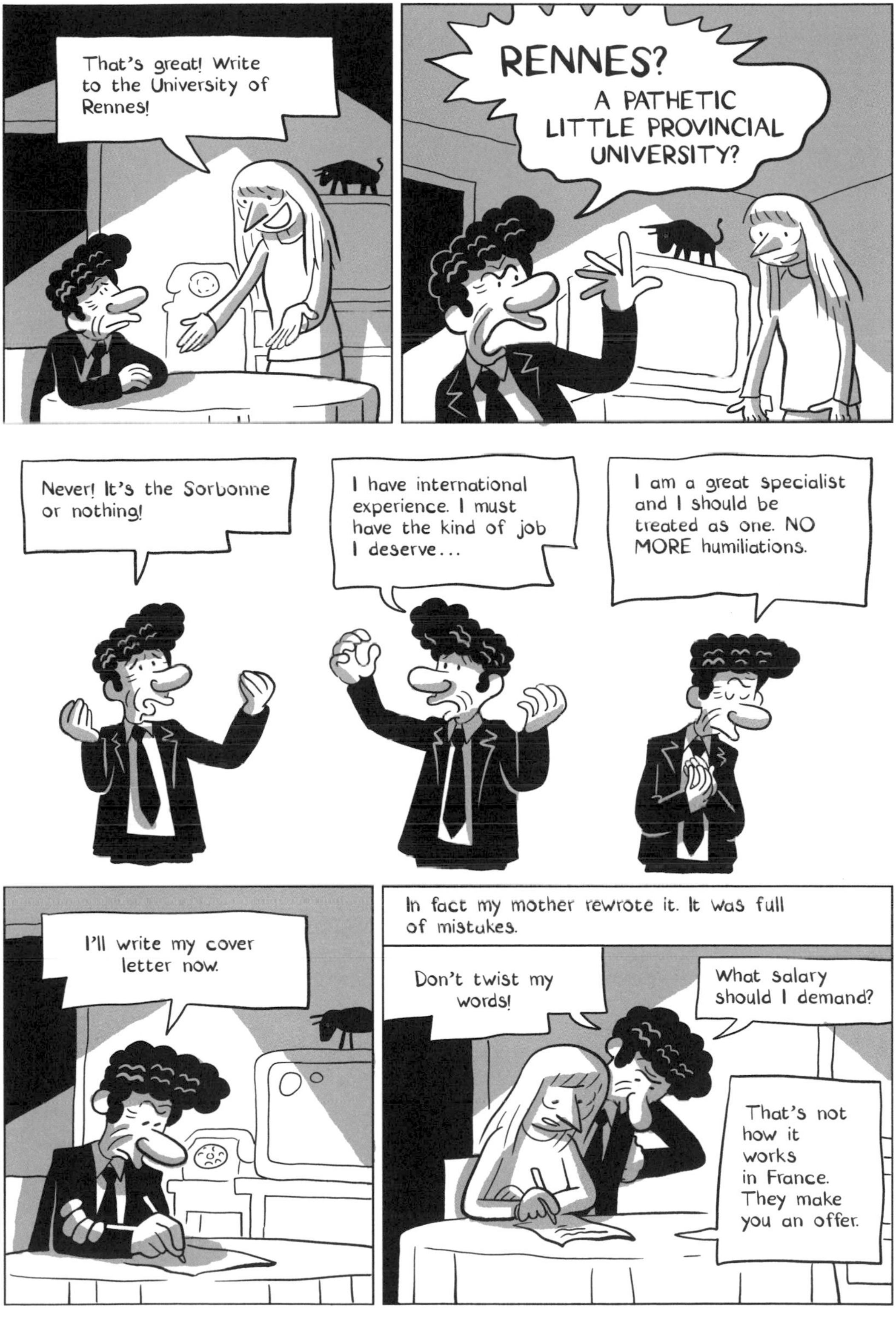

That's great! Write to the University of Rennes!
RENNES? A PATHETIC LITTLE PROVINCIAL UNIVERSITY?
Never! It's the Sorbonne or nothing!
I have international experience. I must have the kind of job I deserve...
I am a great specialist and I should be treated as one. NO MORE humiliations.
I'll write my cover letter now.
In fact my mother rewrote it. It was full of mistakes.
Don't twist my words!
What salary should I demand?
That's not how it works in France. They make you an offer.

We were going on a family vacation. The treatment had worked and my mother was better. My father had not heard back from the Sorbonne, but everybody was happy.

My mother had agreed to spend July and August in Syria. The family there hadn't seen us for three years.

I really didn't want to go.

Jewwww!
Jew! Hey! Jew!

I tried to forget by reading video game magazines.

I dreamed of having a computer one day

TILT

I was going to have to pretend to be a believer again so they wouldn't harass me...

I was afraid they wouldn't believe my lies

TILT

The trip went on forever, but our arrival was very different from previous times.

Ahlan doktor!

AAHH doktor...

My father's old student, the one who'd taken us to Lebanon and who'd been one of Assad's "bodyguards," was now the head of a department with the border police.

Come! Come please!

The problems with my father's military service were now in the past.

Whoa! A van just for us!

During the trip from Damascus to Tel Maaleh, I had hallucinations.

BLAM!

I watched as each building we passed exploded.

BLAM!

BLAM!

What's the matter? Are you sick?

NO. IT'S REALLY COOL. EVERYTHING'S EXPLODING!

I IMAGINE THAT EVERYTHING EXPLODES ...AND I REALLY SEE IT!

What's he talking about? There's something wrong with that kid, by God.

I felt like I was much stronger than I had been three years before.

I thought I had grown big enough that I could stop them from bullying me. I was ready to fight.

A light on in my cousins' apartment

The building was badly damaged on the side where our apartment was.

As if someone had attacked the wall

Where are we, Mama?

It still smelled of concrete and oil

AND NOW: TIME TO REST AND HAVE FUN!

OH YEAH!

Nothing had moved in my room in the past three years.

My old toys were covered in dust, and I wasn't interested in them anymore.

If I read and reread my copies of TILT, the time would pass quickly and we would soon be back in France

We had hardly finished unpacking before my father's mood darkened.

He prayed in the living room in front of everybody.

My mother began reading *The Thorn Birds*.

I'm not moving!

Me neither.

On the first night, I heard a strange noise in our bedroom.

FRRRFFRRCRRRRCCCFRRRR
FRRRRRRRRRRFF

?

The next morning we went to see my grandmother.

She covered me in drool.

She sobbed loudly.

OOOH! OOOOOH!

She started talking to my mother.

What did she say?

Nothing—she's very old...

She thinks that France is near Homs.

So she wants to know why you don't come to see her more often.

HA HA HA! She doesn't really think that, does she? HA HA!

Mama, who's the old man in black?

My mother had agreed to come back to Syria on one condition: she was not going to cook any meals or clean the house. She was going to rest.

My father agreed to this. My aunt Khadija would do our laundry and feed us.

My father gave her money, and she and her daughters did the cooking

Everybody seemed to talk about me all the time. They looked at me strangely.

What are they saying?

Shaaru muja'ad hala, ktir hilu!

What? You're also asking me "What are they saying?"

Arabic is your language! How can you have forgotten it? You should be ashamed! You think you're French? You're an Arab!

AN ARAB! AN ARAB!

They say you've changed so much that you look like someone else. They don't recognize you now that you're not blond anymore...

Smack!

I'd paid no attention to the way my hair had changed color.

But over time, it had turned brown.

It was now frizzy like this

I wasn't blond at all anymore.

And I hadn't even noticed

Move over a bit.

What would I look like when I was older?

212

I'd never worried about the body I'd have as an adult.

This is how I imagined things changing ───→

I was sorry I'd asked for a different haircut. That was when my hair started turning frizzy and brown.

I'd always imagined that I'd be blond all my life. Now I doubted everything.

What if I didn't get mega-muscular?

What if I wasn't six foot six?

That was when I noticed something moving near the top of the blinds.

SQUEEEK

A tiny little foot!

SQUEEEK

A tiny little foot!

I touched it

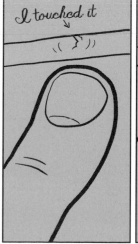

It disappeared

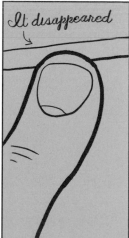

Say hello to your cousin Wael! He's an excellent student, always top of the class! He still talks about you! Mohamed is a big boy now. He looks after the goats in the field. They are both GOOD Muslims.

Anyway, I'll leave you to it. Have fun!

He had changed, too. He was more nervous than before and his face was covered in zits.

Speak Arabic or English?

?

Arabic.

Wael started talking to me as if I understood him.

Tahal tahal!

He took me to his parents' apartment, across the hall.

We started playing marbles...

LEISHE MA SHELEH BOTTU HADA?!

214

Qamar had grown a LOT. She'd become the most beautiful woman I'd ever seen.

Biaamel eli badu yah!!!

LA! LA!

I fell madly and instantly in love with her

She was shouting because I was wearing shoes in her apartment when everybody else took theirs off.

In Ter Maaleh it was common for cousins to marry.

This kept money and family from going elsewhere.

I was completely ready to marry my cousin.

It was the first time I'd felt this way about a real person.

Suddenly I noticed that Qamar and her mother were looking at me.

Wael was yelling at them and taking me outside.

We went near the school. Children were moving about in the tall grass.

One after another, they threw stones at a wasps' nest stuck to a thistle.

THE WASPS ATTACKED!

AARRGGHH!!!

Then it was Wael's turn.

GOD IS GREAT!

He hit it!

Suddenly, in the sky, we saw a huge wasp fly past.

It looked like it belonged to a different species

It went up the street...

...headed toward our house...

...and flew under the roller blinds in my bedroom!

There were lots of others!

A few months before this, looking at a real girl had had no effect on me...

Now I was bewitched, as if someone had put me under an evil spell.

I found it hard to sleep...

Hell awaits you.

...the hornets kept scratching and buzzing.

I was following a woman as she walked past a factory.

Impossible to see her face.

She was a mix of all the women I had ever seen.

I called out to her, but no sound came from my mouth

The faster I ran, the farther away she was.

Then she stopped and began to turn toward me...

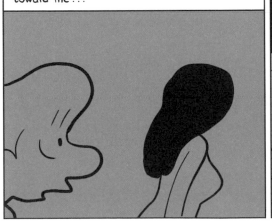

In less than a month, my Arabic came back. It was the summer holidays so there was no school, but every day Wael and Mohamed had to herd their father's goats to a different field to graze.

I went with them sometimes

Temperature: 106 degrees

BAAA

Smell of hay and goat dung

I tried to explain the world of computers to them.

The most powerful computer is the Amiga 3000! It's American. It costs a fortune!

If I ever become rich, by God, I'm going to buy one!

In my opinion, they have more powerful computers in the USSR.

Talking made me desperately thirsty.

My cousins weren't affected

How did they do it?

I always took a small flask of water.

It didn't hold much. I kept it for the way back

One day, we saw another herd.

Look! It's our uncles, by God!

Moktar picked up a rock and started to throw it at me.

HUHHH

Uncle, stop it, by God!

We're family! We mustn't fight!

Look at that son of a bitch being all high and mighty on our land!

You dare come here and act like it's your home! Did you tell him we all know what's going on?

Stop it, Uncle...

The whole village knows that while your father is working in Saudi Arabia, your bitch of a mother is sleeping with a different man every day, using his car!

Grrr!

Wael and Mohamed stopped me. My flask fell to the ground.

SON OF A DOG! A CURSE ON YOUR MOTHER'S FATHER'S MOTHER'S FATHER!

Riad, they're family...

They walked away...

It's true they're a bit crazy, but that's just how it is...

I was thirsty. I decided to go back home as quickly as possible.

It was at least an hour's walk back to the village.

I was so thirsty that I had to stop.

Was I going to collapse like Tintin in the desert?

Suddenly I saw a field of tomatoes.

I lay down in between the plants so the farmers couldn't see me.

I picked an enormous tomato.

It was warm, and its delicious juice was the best thing I had ever tasted

I had never given much thought to how babies were made. Nobody had explained it to me.

I knew that men and women were involved... but how did it happen?

My cousins had a small rabbit farm on the roof of our building.

There were rabbits everywhere, and we spent hours watching them.

Look at its willy! When you do this, you can see it!

HA HA! It looks like a red pepper!

So, that's it! That's how humans make babies, too!!!

You shouldn't talk about that, Riad... It's indecent and forbidden by the sacred laws...

But you knew?

Well, yeah.

The willy has to go in the woman's hole...

Now I understood all the secrets of life.

My father wanted us to stay in Syria. He had never given up on the idea. My mother categorically refused.

At night we stood on the balcony and watched for shooting stars

Papa? How many stars are there in the sky?

An infinite number! There are too many to count.

1...2...3...4...5...

STOP IT!

What?

Stop counting them. It's forbidden by the sacred laws.

If you point at the stars, you'll be covered in warts.

Only God knows how many stars there are. Trying to count them is arrogant. It's like trying to be God, and it's a terrible sin.

WOOOOOOO°

↑ *Warm, straw-scented*

It's getting windy so I'm going to take the washing off the line and then I'm going to bed.

It is a grave sin to try to guess God's plans, Riad! Never forget that!

Know your place, obey your father, and submit to God. You understand?

Um, yeah. I'm going to read TILT.

Suddenly I heard the front door open, and my mother came running inside.

SLAM!!! AHH TAP TAP TAP

What happened?

OH, I WAS SCARED! I WAS SO SCARED!

SOMETHING ATTACKED ME ON THE ROOF!

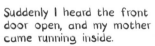

I went up to the roof with my basket. It was windy...

WHOOOO

I was rushing to take the laundry off the line...and then...

?

Showers of sparks flew down from the sky and surrounded me!

I grabbed the basket, turned around, and...

BOOOOOO! A BLACK SHAPE BLEW ON MY FACE! I screamed and ran away! Oh, I was sooo scared!

I had never seen my mother in such a state before.

I'm going up.

There was no wind now

It's Satan. Satan came to see your mother!

Oh God, protect us! Protect us, my God.

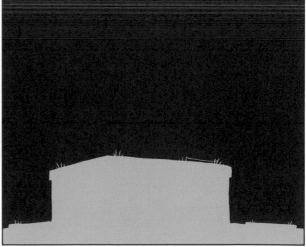

After that incident, my mother didn't want to leave the house.

Where's my Degas print?

Oh, I took it down. It's indecent, a half-naked woman...It will bring us misfortune.

WHAT IS WRONG WITH YOU? GIVE IT BACK NOW!

My father gave it back to her and she packed it in her suitcase.

Degas! A great artist!

What is going on in your head, exactly? You have a PhD from the Sorbonne and you're bothered by a drawing?

THIS IS INSANE!!!

IT'S IN-DE-CENT! IT'S HARAM! AND I'M THE MAN, SO I DECIDE!

THE MAN! WHAT A JOKE!

What do you mean "what a joke"? A WOMAN MUST OBEY HER HUSBAND!

I don't obey anybody! I'm not like the submissive women in your backward village!

Since they were fighting, I went to see Wael and Mohamed.

Ah, Riad! Come on, we're playing Shaddeh.

Sit down, my brother.

No, I'm not playing!

He kept his shoes on again! It's an insult!

I quickly took them off.

Do Wael and Mohamed keep their shoes on when they visit your home?

I, uh—

NO, of course not.

And yet you think it's okay to come into our home with your shoes on. Do you think we're inferior to you? You think the French are better than us?

Their mother arrived. She looked strange.

Riad. I must speak to you about something IMPORTANT.

Listen carefully.

Three years ago, you told my children that your grandparents were friends with a ghost.

Um, I—

That they gave it food and the food disappeared.

That it made plates fly through the air...

Why don't you get rid of it? ANSWER!

Are your grandparents witches, friends of Satan?

I lied! It was a joke... I just said it to scare them, for fun... There's no ghost in my grandparents' house...

HA HA

They had been worrying about that for three years!

232

I knew you were lying! Your eyes are full of trickery and deceit! Your family is a family of evil infidels.

Bah!

Calm down, daughter...

Hey, leave him alone. We were about to play cards!

SHUT UP!

Why don't you pray?

Why have you never gone to see your father in Saudi Arabia?

You could have made your pilgrimage. You're lucky to have family there...and yet you don't go with your father...

And I'm SURE you eat pork!

ADMIT IT!

NO, I DONT!

Sudden desire for sausage

I couldn't get over the perfection of her face. And despite her baggy clothes...

...it was easy to see the curves of her body. She smelled good, too: a mix of sweat and another scent that I couldn't identify.

Be careful, Riad! You know what awaits infidels, the punishment reserved for them by God, if that is his will...

The flames of Hell, of course.

How would she ever agree to marry me if she hated me so much?

I knew it was illogical to love someone who despised me, but it was beyond my control.

What would happen if I did marry her? As my father always said, a Syrian woman would follow me everywhere. So we would go to France.

Oooh, is that a minaret?

Uh, it's Cap Fréhel.

People would find her clothes strange and give her dirty looks...

Don't any of these Christians hide their hair from men?

...And she would always be outraged by people's free and easy morals.

ARGH these infidels kissing in public! A CURSE ON THEIR MOTHERS' FATHERS!

She wouldn't be able to stand the sound of church bells.

DONG DONG DING

Where is the mosque? Why haven't we been called to prayer?

She would refuse to buy meat at the butcher's.

The knife that cut the pork is the same that cuts the beef!

And the beef is not halal! I WON'T EAT IT!

I would try to convince her to live like a Frenchwoman, to take off her veil...

I feel uncomfortable.

...And she'd instantly be seen as the most beautiful girl in the country.

I imagined her in jeans...

These infidel pants are too tight.

...in a dress.

How indecent! A Jew's dress!

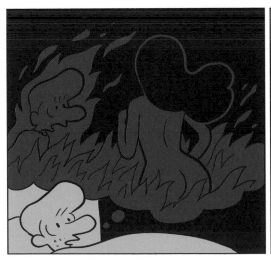

I felt sure I would be punished for my impure thoughts.

CRR CRR VVVV CR CR CR CR CR CR CRCK CR

Sometime later...

The wasps hurled themselves at the window.

I was worried that the window might give way.

I went to lie down next to my mother on the balcony.

My mother was asleep. She looked less tired than before. I could tell she wasn't sick anymore.

CRACK

What the...I don't believe it...did someone just... what the—

A HUGE ROCK HAD LANDED LESS THAN TWO INCHES FROM HER FACE!

She realized that if that rock had landed on her face ...

... she might have been killed!

FILTHY JEWS! A CURSE ON YOU! A CURSE ON YOUR JEWISH MOTHER'S MOTHER'S FATHER! SLUT! A CURSE ON YOUR GOD! I'LL KILL YOU ALL!

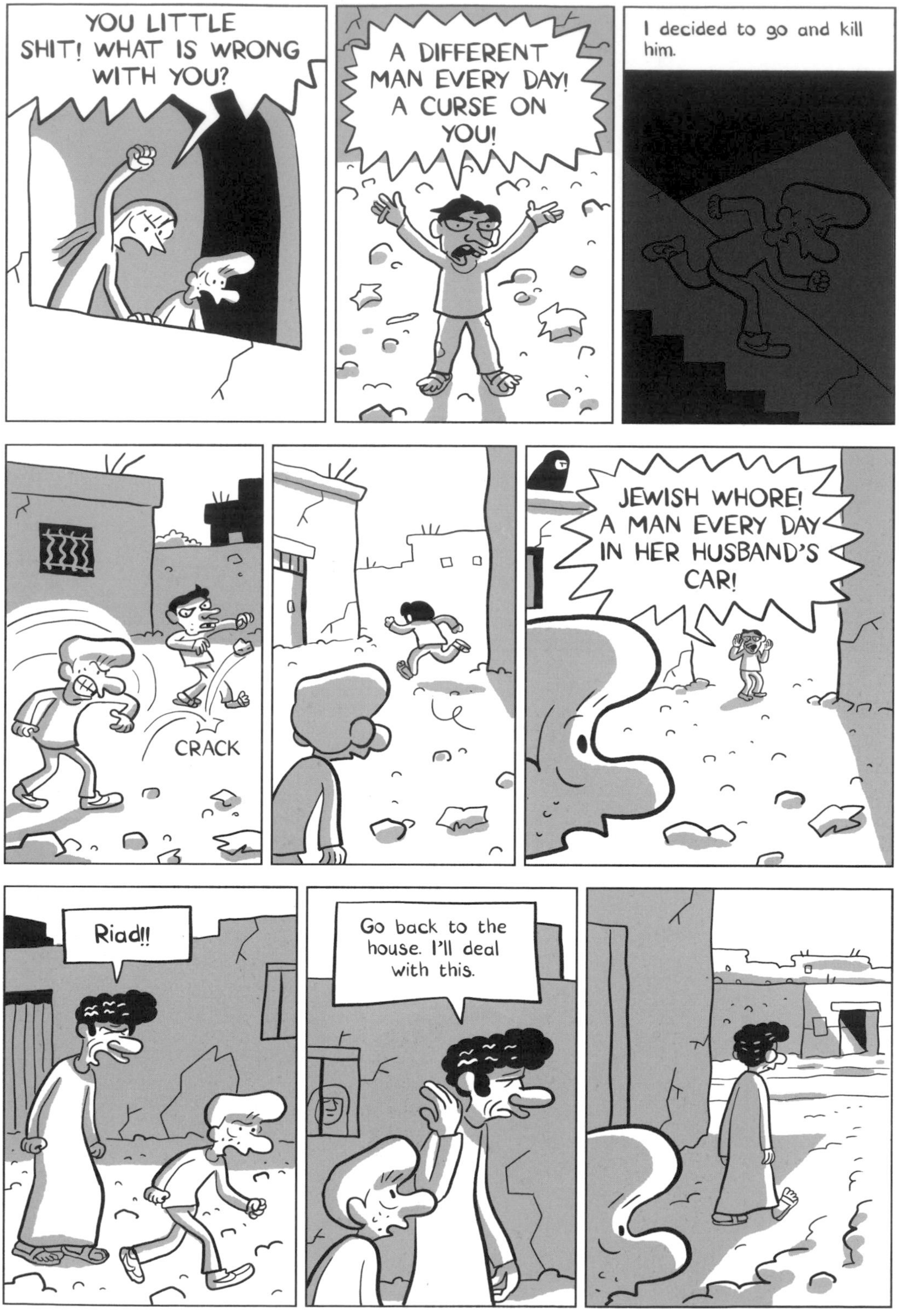
YOU LITTLE SHIT! WHAT IS WRONG WITH YOU?
A DIFFERENT MAN EVERY DAY! A CURSE ON YOU!
I decided to go and kill him.
CRACK
JEWISH WHORE! A MAN EVERY DAY IN HER HUSBAND'S CAR!
Riad!!
Go back to the house. I'll deal with this.

My father headed toward my grandmother's house, where Anas's father, Hadj Mohamed, lived.

He came out a few minutes later with Hadj Mohamed.

He took the leather belt from his jelabah and let the buckle drag along the ground.

It had been a long time since I last saw him.

His eyes stared coldly ahead

He went to find his son ...

Happy to imagine how Anas would suffer

Go! Back in the house, Riad! Stop trying to be a cowboy! GO HOME!

My brother will deal with him now, by God.

Thanks to his high-ranking friend, my father was hired as an associate professor at the University of Damascus.

I DON'T CARE IF YOU STAY HERE!

I'm taking the children home.

I want to work so I can retire one day! I haven't had a job in fifteen years. I'm going to end up old and poor!

But most of all I can't stand this country. I can't stand this way of life! I don't want to be killed by some teenage degenerate.

I'VE HAD IT UP TO HERE WITH ARABS!

ACH! RACIST! THAT'S RACIST! YOU'RE A RACIST, LIKE ALL FRENCH PEOPLE!

LIKE YOU, YOU MEAN!

YOU NEVER STOP CURSING THE JEWS, THE BLACKS, THE FRENCH, THE CHRISTIANS, ALL DAY LONG! TAKE A LOOK IN THE MIRROR! A PHD IN HISTORY AND YOU'RE UPSET BY DEGAS'S DANCERS! IT'S PATHETIC! HA HA

IT'S DEPRESSING, ALL YOUR PRAYERS AND SUPERSTITIONS!

YOU USED TO BE SO MODERN, BUT LOOK AT YOU NOW!

YOU'RE LIKE YOUR MOTHER!

The battery's the wrong way around, that's all.

Well, there's only one solution. I'm going to marry another woman! That way I'll have one here and one in France!

♪ "We'll go wherever you like whenever you like"

Go ahead! Honestly, feel free! Be like your brother, with his two wives!

Your religion condones it! It's the next logical step, in fact...

I was kidding...

Well, I'M not! If that's what it takes to make you happy! I'll marry someone else, too—a Frenchman!

Huh?

As long as I don't have to live in this village with your inbred family, everything will be great.

"Inbred"? What's that mean?

It means "people in the same family who sleep together, producing retarded children"! That's what "inbred" means!

TILT

That day, we went to eat lunch at my aunt's house.

As usual, my father talked about his mystical experience.

Religion is all that matters. We must follow God.

Oh yes! Oh yes.

Yes, by God.

Cursed are those who distance themselves from God! Cursed are those who try to find happiness with infidels and unbelievers.

Cursed are those who deny their faith to live like an infidel.

Only God knows what must happen and when it must happen. Only God decides, only God knows the reasons for everything. CURSED are those who do not respect God!

HM.

HM.

My mother asked him to translate what he had just said.

I said: "Cursed be they who do not respect God!"'

WAHAHAHAHA! WHAT A LOAD OF CRAP!

?

sniffff

FSHTT!

ARRGGHH

ΛΛHH

WHO'S LAUGHING NOW?

ARE YOU **CRAZY?** WHY DID YOU **DO** THAT?

IN FRONT OF **THE KIDS!**

GOD IS NO LAUGHING MATTER!

HES CRAZY!
HE'S CRAZY!

My father took us home in silence.

My mother locked herself in her bedroom.

Go to your rooms!

I want to see Mama.

Later...

I need to talk to her.

She yelled at my father for an hour, calling him every name under the sun. Then things calmed down.

I'm sorry, I'm sorry. I lost it when you laughed at God, but... I'm so sorry...

My mother said nothing else.

She left her room to make some tea

She was limping slightly

Three days later she packed our suitcases. The vacation was over.

Time to go hooome!

This was the happiest she'd seemed all summer.

Pick up all the books and toys that you want to take back to France...

Who knows when we'll be here again!

My father was haunted by guilt for having burned her foot.

I'm going to take my Tintins.

He rubbed his forehead and stared at the wall...

...then his gaze grew hard and cold...

...he stared at the floor.

When will you come and see us, Papa?

I have classes to teach. Maybe at Christmas? Or in the spring? Soon.

Quick, we'll miss the bus!

No, no, it won't be here for another 40 minutes... We have time...

It was obvious that my mother was glad my father was staying in Syria.

The customs officers at the airport carried our luggage for us.

My mother refused to kiss my father.

He kissed me and inhaled deeply.

SNFF
Smick
SNFFF
Smick

CHAPTER 9

My mother found a part-time job as a secretary.

In the morning, she walked my two brothers to school.

Mama! I'm your husband! Eh, Mama?

Yes, baby, you are!

Then she came back to pick up the car and drove to work.

I went on my own to the middle school

The street smelled of rain

I was in love with three girls I saw on the bus every morning.

I knew the way each of them smelled.

Detergent

Eau Jeune perfume

Sweet sweat

My father was still in Syria. We hadn't heard from him in nearly a year.

I didn't think about him much anymore because there wasn't room in my brain

I was in eighth grade. Vanessa and Céline, my old friends from sixth grade, had voted me the ugliest boy in the class.

I was terrified each morning when I arrived at school

The one above me in the ranking was a mentally handicapped boy named Louis-Henri.

I was slightly more handsome than him, frankly

GRNT

Céline and Vanessa belonged to a group of popular kids from good families (shopkeepers, doctors) who were tall, good-looking, and well fed.

They had torrid romantic lives

Most envious boy on earth

Titouan was one of their leaders. He'd grown and was very athletic. He went from girl to girl.

There were parties every weekend, and I was never invited

Hey, Mr. Pubes ...

Da widdle wabbit ...

At lunchtime I ate with two outcast but ultra-smart boys who let me sit at their table.

Nicolas and Sébastien

In the Middle Ages, even the children were crucified by the lords.

Yeah, that must have hurt ...

After lunch they played tag under the trees. I went with them.

Hee hee

Hee hee hee

But they ran after each other and forgot about me

I still dreamed of having a computer. I was kind of friends with a boy who had an Amiga 500. His name was Grégory.

His family had a nice house with a garden, and he had a computer, but he complained about being poor.

I played Turrican all weekend. You know it?

Yeah, TILT gave it six stars for the graphics, animation, music...

It was really great...

Look at all those rich kids...

We need a revolution to change society...

He was extremely handsome but had a dark view of life.

He wasn't part of the popular group but he'd been ranked one of the best-looking boys in the class.

Girls hate me.

But it's all right. I've accepted the idea that I'll never go out with a girl in my life. It's fine...

OK

Céline and Vanessa did that only to make fun of me, that's obvious...

But I noticed that half the girls in the school were fascinated by him.

I would have given anything to be him, to live his life...

HE HAD THE BODY I SHOULD HAVE HAD!

Bullshit, man, no way ha ha...I'm too ugly...

Fuck it...I'll never get a girl...

251

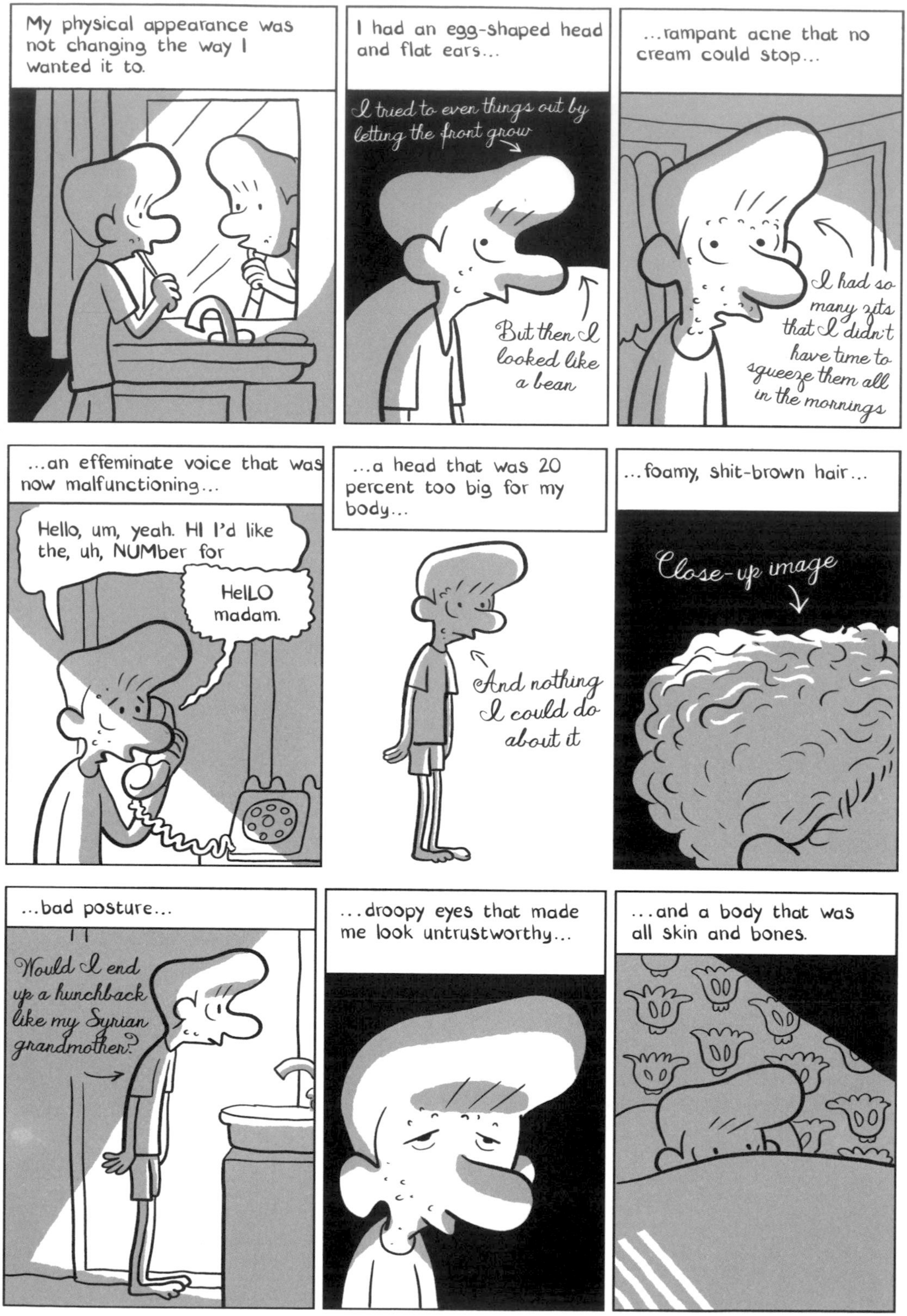
My physical appearance was not changing the way I wanted it to.
I had an egg-shaped head and flat ears...
I tried to even things out by letting the front grow
But then I looked like a bean
...rampant acne that no cream could stop...
I had so many zits that I didn't have time to squeeze them all in the mornings
...an effeminate voice that was now malfunctioning...
Hello, um, yeah. HI I'd like the, uh, NUMber for
HelLO madam.
...a head that was 20 percent too big for my body...
And nothing I could do about it
...foamy, shit-brown hair...
Close-up image
...bad posture...
Would I end up a hunchback like my Syrian grandmother?
...droopy eyes that made me look untrustworthy...
...and a body that was all skin and bones.

One day, my hip really hurt. My mother took me to get an X-ray.

Let's take a look... a lot of people in Brittany have bad hips...

Let's see...

I hope it's nothing serious.

Hm...I don't see anything unusual. In my opinion these are just growing pains... You see this space here?

Above the bone?

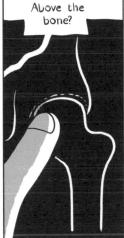

That's where you still have to grow.

Really? So... am I going to be...TALL?

Nah, not really...

Maybe another inch or so.

My grandfather and his girlfriend, Brigitte, came to see us.

They smelled of sunscreen

For unknown reasons, Brigitte acted differently toward me than she had the first time I'd met her...

She stared at me coldly

So, shall we go shopping?

My mother had not told anyone about my father burning her foot.

CARREFOUR

What's Abdel up to? Why doesn't he come and live in France?

I don't know and I don't care!

We're better off without him!

Yeah, but the kids need a father!

The boys will end up queer without a dad! Riad is already borderline, with his girly voice and his obsession with art.

Three little fags in the family, that's all we need...

Uggh, Papa, stop...

Whoa! Boys, check out that photographer! Come on, let's get our picture taken. It'll give us something to remember!

PHOTO SOUVENI

TAND

YVES ROCH

Okay, boys. Keep still and say "Cheeese"!

CHEEEEEEESE!

CLICK

I'm going to put this picture in my kitchen. That way I'll see you every day!

?!?

The next day, my grandfather took me to school in his car.

Riad, what did you do to Brigitte? She HATES you!

Really?

It's weird, because she likes most people...

Did you say something?

No, nothing!

It must be the way you look.

Don't worry about it. Women can be just as stupid and annoying as men...

Ooh, there are some pretty girls in your school!

Hey, how's it going, Mr. Pubes?

Ha ha

Why did so many people hate me for no reason?

One spring evening a few months later, the doorbell rang.

SURPRIIIIISE!

He'd aged, and his accent had grown stronger.

I brought you some presents!

A He-Man for Yahya.

Some Legos for Fadi.

And for Riad, a Quran. But you don't have to read it.

And for Clémentine, this beautiful, very heavy pure gold necklace!

No, thanks. I don't want it!

Okay, no problem! I'll get you something else!

No, I don't want anything. Oh, except for some warning next time you're coming.

AAAAAH. Well, I'M really happy to see you all again!

You're my papa, right?

Can you buy me a Game Boy next time?

He'd changed. He didn't pray anymore, and he was very gentle.

Yep, I'm modern again!

Good for you.

He'd even started drinking wine again.

Mmm, Côtes du Rhône is soooo nice!

My favorite wine!

It was obvious that he wanted to show us he'd changed.

When I was a student, I used to deliver newspapers...

...and I had lots of Jewish customers! I'd arrive outside their nice apartments and shout...

...HELLOOO! IT'S ME, YOUR LITTLE ARAB COUSIN! I'VE BROUGHT YOUR PAPER!

How they'd laugh! They used to give me good tips.

They were really very nice, those Jews...

My father did nothing all day. When I came home from school on the bus...

...he'd be waiting for me on the corner.

Let me carry your bag!

No, it's fine...

C'mon, I want to.

Is there anything you need?

No, I'm going to do my homework.

Okay, I'll go back to bed.

He spent most of his time lying on the bed in the dark.

When my mother came home from work, she ignored him.

You want me to go to the bakery?

No, its fine. I already did the shopping.

He tried to help, but she didn't want him to.

OUT OF MY WAY!

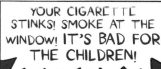

I want half of the Jersey money! I earned it just as much as you did!

YOUR CIGARETTE STINKS! SMOKE AT THE WINDOW! IT'S BAD FOR THE CHILDREN!

Mghmgh wallaheuu uuu

Our family walks in the center of Rennes always ended the same way.

My father tried to hold my mother's hand...

GET OFF ME!

BUT I'M YOUR HUSBAND!

PFFT! YOU'RE A USELESS LUMP!

They'd argue, and everybody would stop and watch.

I'd slip away. I didn't want to be seen with them.

My mother would go back to the car with my brothers, and I'd wait for my father, who'd walk with me in his too-short pants.

260

I was the first one up in the morning.

6:30 am

I often saw my father in the kitchen.

Smell of cigarette smoke

Listen!

Listen.

Isn't it pretty, what the birds are singing?

They sing in the night.

What time do you finish? I'll come to meet you at the bus stop.

No, don't bother.

I don't have anything else to do...

All right... 4:30...

My mother called her mother every night.

She locked herself in the bedroom so nobody could hear.

One night, while she was on the phone, I heard her rush out into the hallway.

WHAT ARE YOU DOING?

Nothing!

?

Earphones

TILT

Were you listening in on my call? I heard a noise on the line. I know you were spying on me! What were you doing near the phone jack?

NOTHING!

I WASN'T DOING INYTHING!

CLICK!

I'm sure he was listening!

I plugged the earphones into the phone jack in the hallway, to test it.

It worked! I could hear the dial tone through the earphones!

Where did he learn a trick like that?

My mother kept accusing my father of not paying for his children. Finally he exploded.

I don't pay? Me? Riad, what do you want? Tell me anything you want, and I'll buy it for you.

Um, a pair of Adidas Torsion sneakers.

Is that all? Just shoes?

THAT'S NOTHING! MORE!

Say something else MORE EXPENSIVE!

Suddenly I thought of the most wonderful, extraordinary thing in the world, the thing I wanted more than anything else, and it cost 3,490 francs.

Um, well, I would really like an Amiga 500...

What's that? How much?

3,490 francs.

COME ON! LET'S GO TO FNAC!

First my father bought me the sneakers...

800 francs!

This is what I should do with my beautiful DOLLARS!

...Then an Amiga 500!

That computer was the most wonderful thing I had ever seen.

SCRAPE

My money is all for my children!

It's my money, too!

Anybody touches my computer, they're dead, okay?

It's true I've been too stingy recently. And we need to have fun as a family.

So, I have a surprise for you.

I'm inviting you to...

EURO DISNEY! THE WORLD OF DREAMS! IT JUST OPENED!!!

We're all going there for our next vacation, I'VE DECIDED!

YEAH!

My mother refused to go. She stayed in Rennes with Fadi.

Yahya and I would spend a whole day at Euro Disney.

We had to wait for hours. The lines were full of foreigners.

Ma que! Was ich klinge. Ha ha ha.

Mamaaa Lucio! Lucio! Si prego!

THE WAIT TIME FROM HERE IS: 2 hrs 20 mins

Look at this! Anyone would think we were in Libya ...

Smell of sweat

The rides were fun, but way too short.

WOOO

We slept in a Disney hotel.

The next day, my father took us to Paris.

It was very noisy, and it smelled of exhaust fumes

TOOT
VRRR

We started with the Sorbonne, where my father had studied.

Ahh! What bittersweet memories! I spent the best years of my life here...

until that cursed day at the university cafeteria when I met your mother. Ha ha ha, just joking.

Then he took us to a bank.

He didn't show us the photos of girls that he supposedly kept here.

I picked up a few gold bars. Hee hee.

From there, we walked to Opéra, where he left us in a bookstore...

I have something to do next door, back soon.

Pick out a few books— my gift!

FRAZETTA

When he returned, he bought us each a comic book. A Quick & Flupke for my brother and a cartoon adaptation of Conan the Destroyer for me.

I chose it because of the painting on the cover

CONAN

Next, we walked up the Champs-Elysées.

The biggest traffic jam I had ever seen

City of light, my ass...

PFFFT

266

I wanted to go to a video game store that existed only in Paris.

Ooooh, I can't go any farther...

We're almost there!!

It was in a mall near the Arc de Triomphe.

Go ahead. I'll wait for you outside. I'm so tired, I have to sit down for a minute...

Later!

I looked at the games. They were amazing but very expensive.

I went out to find my father, hoping to talk him into buying me one.

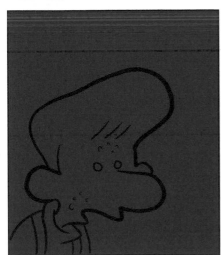

Mgnn mgmn

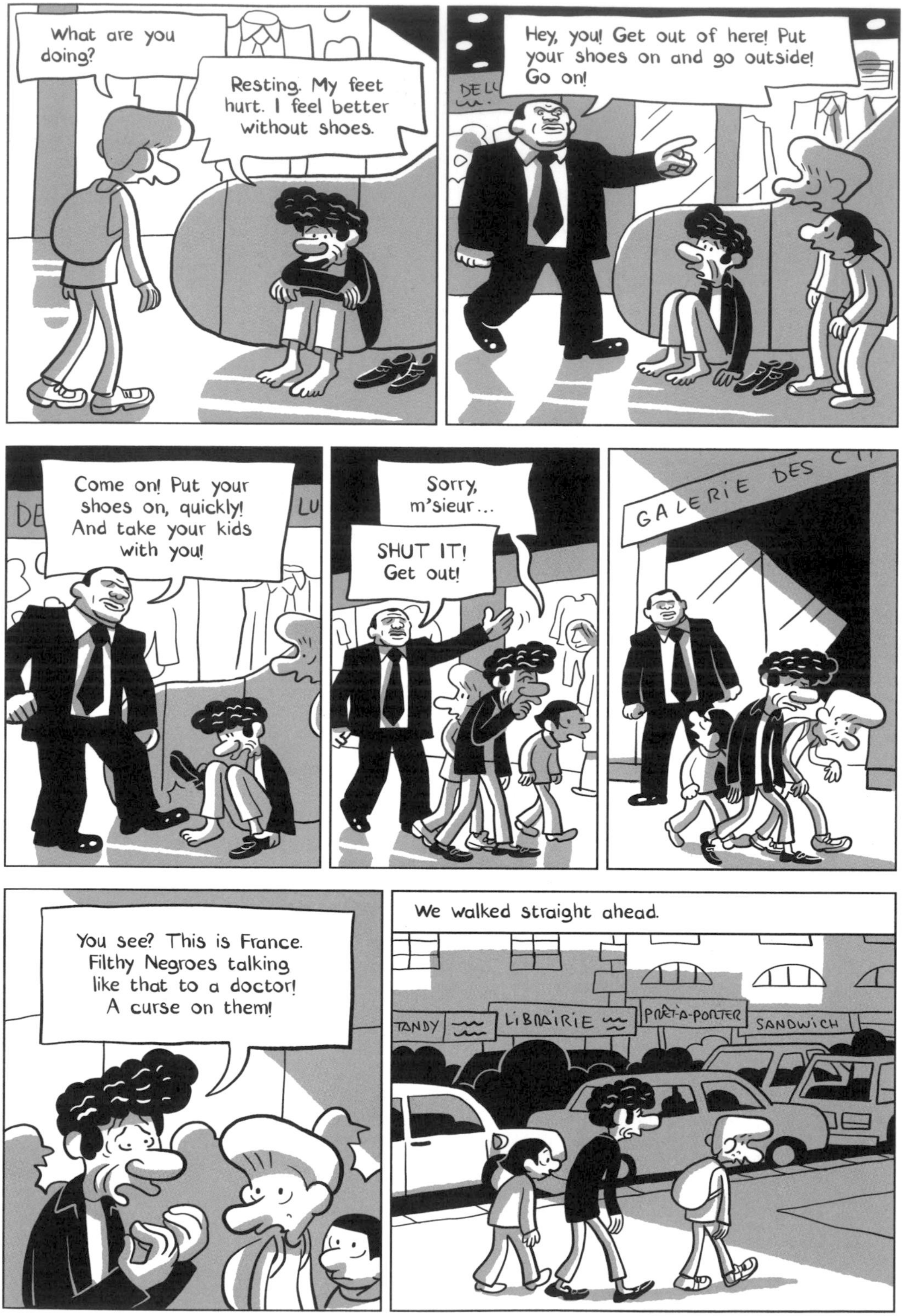
What are you doing?
Resting. My feet hurt. I feel better without shoes.
Hey, you! Get out of here! Put your shoes on and go outside! Go on!
DELI
Come on! Put your shoes on, quickly! And take your kids with you!
Sorry, m'sieur...
SHUT IT! Get out!
GALERIE DES
You see? This is France. Filthy Negroes talking like that to a doctor! A curse on them!
We walked straight ahead.
TANDY
LIBRAIRIE
PRÊT-À-PORTER
SANDWICH

We walked along Boulevard Barbès.

AHHHH, smell that! I love the smell here! It's like being in Homs!

CHEZ OMAR

The sidewalk was black and sticky like in Homs.

Hee hee, we're home now. This is our family! Hee hee! Look at all our cousins!

HEY, COUSIN, HOW ARE YOU?

I'm good hamdullah!

Look at that stupid illiterate North African! He's happy now!

Then we had to take the Métro to the Montparnasse train station. My father wanted to save money, so we all went through the turnstile together.

QUICK, COME ON!

CLAK!

Hello everybody, tickets please!

Hello

Hello

MONSIEUR, TICKETS PLEASE.

It's okay, I'm with my children. Just let us pass...

CONT

NO, IT'S NOT OKAY! YOU SHALL NOT PASS! Stand aside, monsieur. Don't move.

CONT

One of the inspectors looked Arab. My father signaled to him.

?

Pssst! Ya saidi.

24F

My father started whispering to him in Arabic. I couldn't understand what he was saying.

The inspector listened carefully

Go ahead...

Whatcha doing?

It's okay, let them go...

Hee hee, that's how you save money on tickets.

What did you say to him?

Nothing...

ALL Arabs are cousins. Remember that, Riad.

The Jews always help one another. We Arabs should do the same. And in three generations, France will be Arab. You'll understand one day.

We got on the train.

So? Did you enjoy our boys' outing?

It's good being boys together, huh?

YEAH!

If we lived in Syria, we'd be living this life of luxury all the time.

Wouldn't you like to live in Syria with Papa, Mama, and Fadi?

Nah...I prefer France ...There are Amiga games and there aren't any power cuts. The teachers don't beat us...

Me too! And I'm scared of wasps...

Why don't you live in France with us?

You could teach at a university... It'd be great.

Riad. I learned something in Saudi Arabia: God exists. I mean he really exists. Like you and me.

Everything that happens in life is decided by him, and him alone. It is written. Our destiny is written. There is no point in struggling. Only he decides where and when things happen.

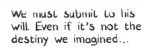

We must submit to his will. Even if it's not the destiny we imagined...

...and now I'm thinking that his will is for us to live in France together.

Your mother is right.

REALLY?

YES!!!

It's not what I would have chosen, but if you all prefer to live in this country full of Negroes... THAT'S FINE! THAT'S FINE! Ha ha ha ha ha ha!

271

The days that followed were very pleasant.

My father announced to my mother that he was going to look for a job in France.

Great.

And he started doing everything at home.

PERU

The shopping, the cooking, the cleaning...

This is like being on vacation...

He took my brothers to school...

I walked along the avenue, heart open to the sky so blue...

...and picked them up in the afternoons.

We'll go wherever you like whenever you like.

HA HA. Is Joe Dassin your father or is it me?

He waited for me at the bus stop so he could carry my bag...

He no longer lay in bed in the dark.

He admired my drawings.

It's beautiful! Look at that, the first Sattouf artist in history!

BRAVO, MY SON!

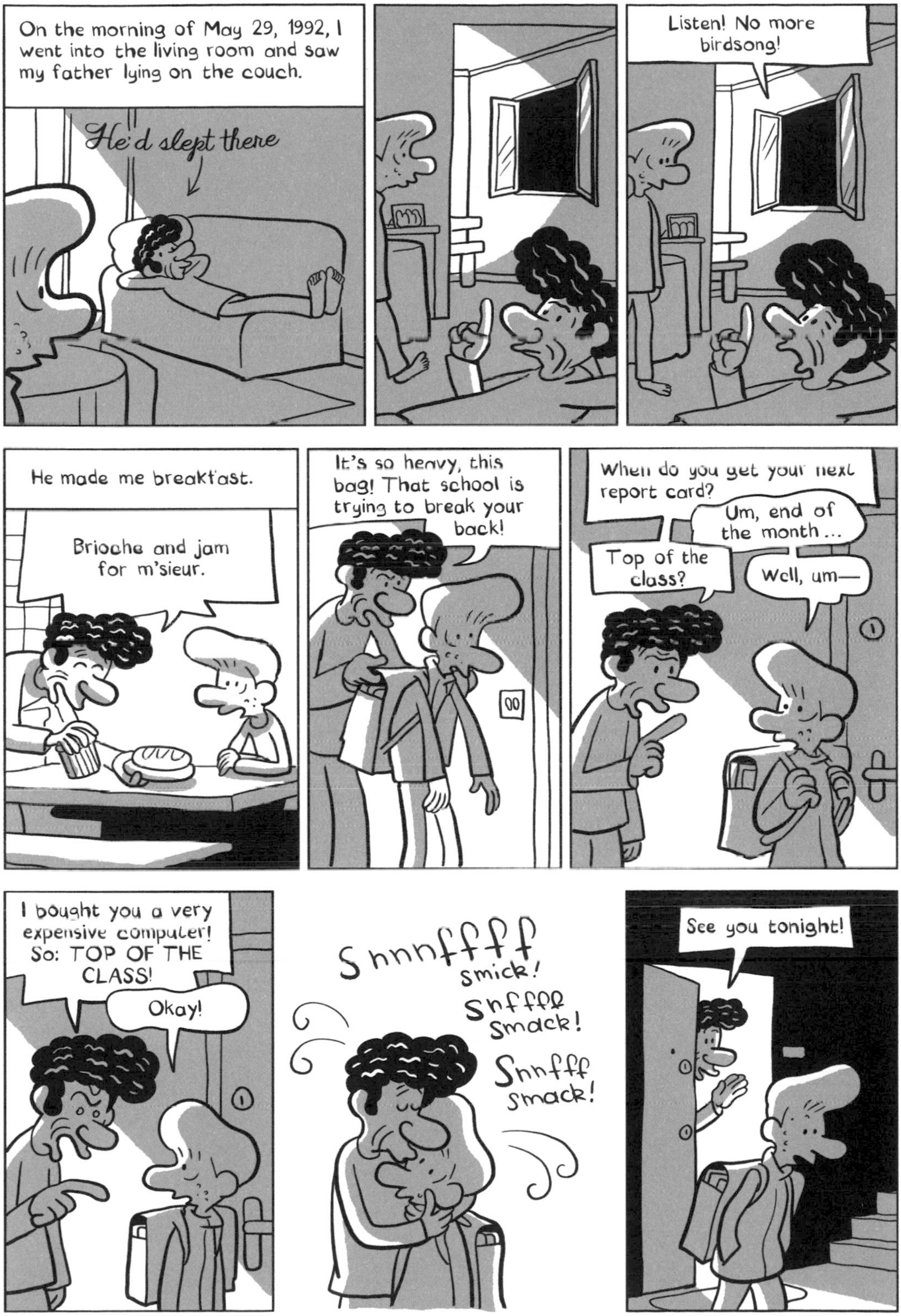
On the morning of May 29, 1992, I went into the living room and saw my father lying on the couch.
He'd slept there
Listen! No more birdsong!
He made me breakfast.
Brioche and jam for m'sieur.
It's so heavy, this bag! That school is trying to break your back!
When do you get your next report card?
Um, end of the month...
Top of the class?
Well, um—
I bought you a very expensive computer! So: TOP OF THE CLASS!
Okay!
Snnffff
smick!
Snffff
smack!
Snnfff
smack!
See you tonight!

The day went by as usual.

Hey, there, Mr. Pubes!

Da widdle wabbit behind da moped...

You're wearing Torsions! Been doing sports, have you?

SMACK

I traded pirated Amiga games with Grégory.

So here is Speedball 2

Treating me as his equal

Shit, I've been thinking about something: so he gave you an Amiga for no reason? It wasn't your birthday or Christmas or whatever?

Uh, right!

So, in fact, you're a big fat BOURGEOIS pig!

JEEZ!

We had a math test.

Grn

In the cafeteria, I sat with Nicolas and Sébastien.

They had given each other nicknames ↘

AH NO, KROZ!

Oh yes, Boz, you're wrong!

In the afternoon I was bored.

Then I took the bus home.

My father was not waiting on the corner

speedball 2

Do you know where your father and Fadi are?

?

He didn't take Fadi to school this morning... Nobody has seen them ...But he took the car and went with him somewhere.

Maybe they're shopping?

275

It was a Friday. By nightfall, my father and Fadi still hadn't come home.

Where ARE they?

THE BULL'S GONE!

I remembered that my father had kissed me while breathing in my scent that morning...

That meant that he was leaving for a long time ↓

Srfff Smick!   Srfff Smick!

Hang on, I, um...I...

We went to the closest police station, in the Blosne neighborhood of Rennes.

What do you mean, "He's kidnapped my son?" Who kidnapped him?

HIS FATHER!!! You have to act quickly, he might have...He's only five, he's a baby...

His father?

Listen, madame. It's Friday night, and there's nobody here. Anyway, you're not divorced?

No, but—

Ah, not divorced! What do you expect us to do?

He can take his son wherever he likes—it's his son! We can't stop him! You understand?

All right, now go home.

My mother tried to argue, but there was nothing to be done. The policeman was not going to tell anyone that my brother was gone.

Besides, maybe you're worrying for no reason. He might bring the kid back...

RING

Hello? Ah, Eric! So?

Uh yeah.

52

My mother sat on my bed and stared out the window for a long time. She was watching the street.

You know, boys, it's not easy, but I'm going to have to divorce your father.

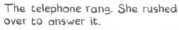

The telephone rang. She rushed over to answer it.

Hello? **WHERE ARE YOU?**

IN JERSEY? WHAT THE HELL ARE YOU DOING IN JERSEY?!

WHY DIDN'T YOU TELL ME? LET ME SPEAK TO FADI!

Hello? My baby, are you okay? Where are you?

A GAME BOY? He bought you a Game Boy?

A Game Boy and lots of toys? That's nice... Soon, you'll be coming home soon! Let me speak to your father!

I'M GOING TO DIVORCE YOU WHEN YOU GET BACK! IT'S OVER!

SLAM!!

My mother alerted my grandmother and Charles, who came right away.

They'll be back, don't worry.

On Saturday, we didn't leave the apartment.

My mother spent the whole day at the window.

She was hoping to see the car appear at the end of the street

I didn't think I'd be able to fall asleep that night, but I did.

I dreamed I was walking past the big factory.

I went into the building.

It was like a labyrinth.

I knew this place

This was where the bulls had charged at me!

I walked forward to see the beast...

...and found myself in an empty room.

I looked behind me, but I had no idea now where I'd come from.

So I took the first escalator.

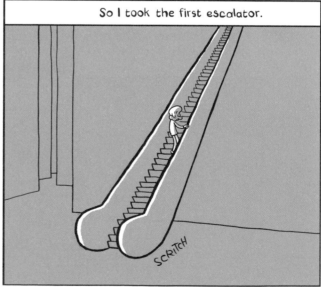

On Sunday, they still weren't back.

My mother returned to the police station, where they told her the same thing.

INCOMPETENT!

That's enough insults now! Go home and don't come back!

She sat in front of the window again, hoping to see the Golf appear.

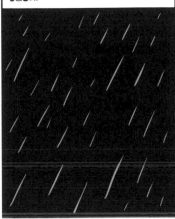

On Sunday evening the phone rang.

It was my father.

An Arab operator connected them

He'd emptied all the bank accounts, including the one in Jersey, and he'd taken my brother with him...

...to Syria.

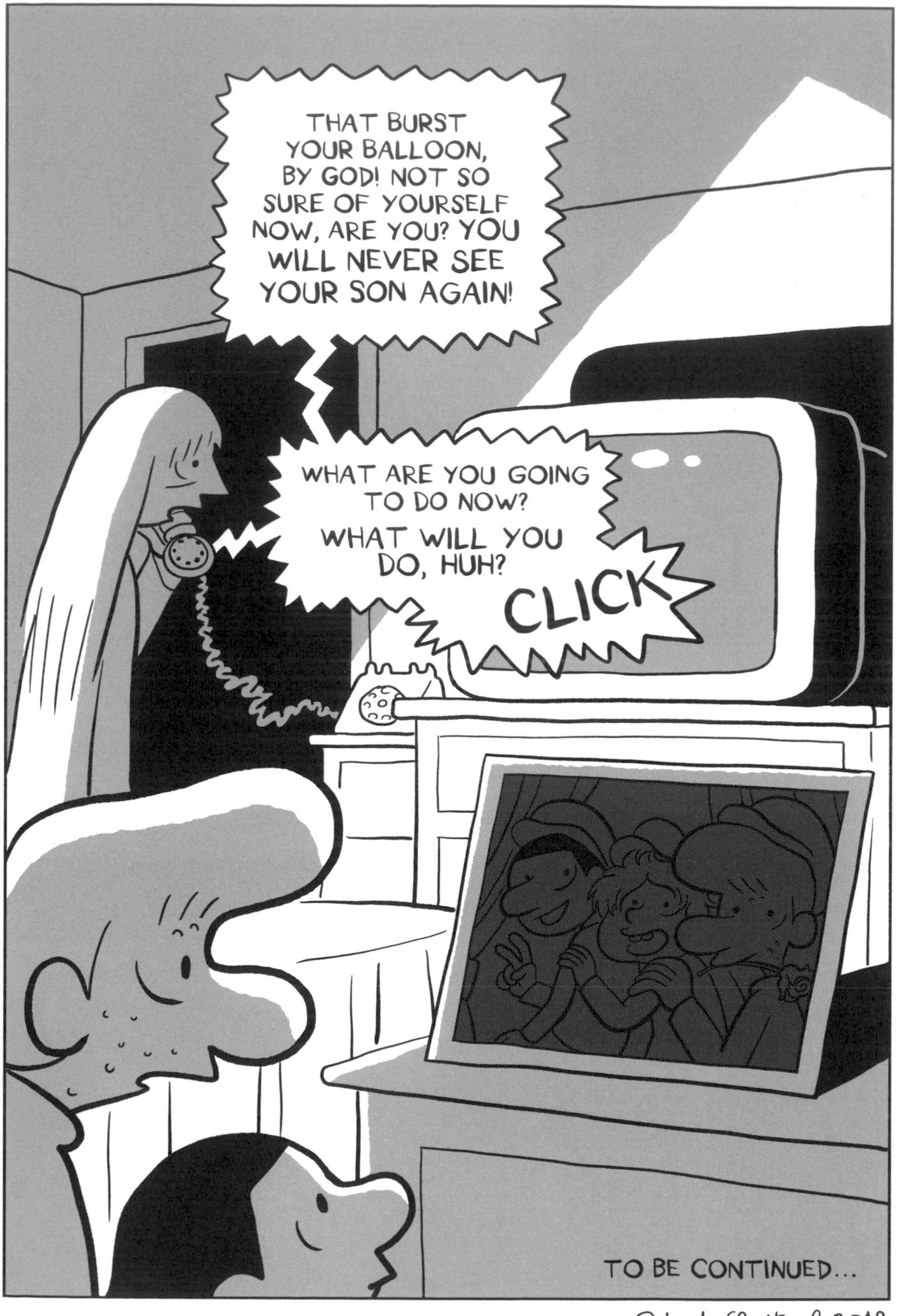
THAT BURST YOUR BALLOON, BY GOD! NOT SO SURE OF YOURSELF NOW, ARE YOU? YOU WILL NEVER SEE YOUR SON AGAIN!
WHAT ARE YOU GOING TO DO NOW?
WHAT WILL YOU DO, HUH?
CLICK
TO BE CONTINUED...

Riad Sattouf 2018

ABOUT THE AUTHOR

RIAD SATTOUF is the author of the bestselling *Arab of the Future* series, which has been translated into twenty-two languages. For the first volume, he received the Angoulême Prize for Best Graphic Novel and the *Los Angeles Times* Book Prize. He grew up in Syria and Libya and now lives in Paris. A former contributor to the satirical publication *Charlie Hebdo*, Sattouf is now a weekly columnist for *L'Obs*. He has also written three other comics series in France and directed the films *The French Kissers* and *Jacky in the Women's Kingdom*.